Śrī Caitanya Mahāprabhu

Other Publications from Bhakti Vikas Trust

Books by His Holiness Bhakti Vikāsa Swami

A Beginner's Guide to Kṛṣṇa Consciousness
A Message to the Youth of India
Brahmacarya in Kṛṣṇa Consciousness
Glimpses of Traditional Indian Life
Jaya Śrīla Prabhupāda!
Lekha-mālā
Mothers and Masters
My Memories of Śrīla Prabhupāda
On Pilgrimage in Holy India
On Speaking Strongly in Śrīla Prabhupāda's Service
Patropadeśa (two volumes)
Rāmāyaṇa
Śrī Bhaktisiddhānta Vaibhava (three volumes)
Śrī Vaṁśīdāsa Bābājī
The Story of Rasikānanda
Gauḍīya Vaiṣṇava Padyāvalī (Bengali)
Vaiṣṇava Śikhā o Sādhana (Bengali)

Books by Other Authors

Śrī Cāṇakya-nīti (by Patita Pāvana Dāsa Adhikārī)
Rethinking Darwin (by Lalitānātha Dāsa)
Who is Supreme? (by Gokula Candra Dāsa)
Viveka-śatakam (by Prabodhānanda Sarasvatī)
How I Achieved Real Success (by Indira Meshram)

All glories to Śrī Guru and Śrī Gaurāṅga

Śrī Caitanya Mahāprabhu

Bhakti Vikāsa Swami

Bhakti Vikas Trust

Śrī Caitanya Mahāprabhu (English)
ISBN 978-81-902332-5-5

Previous printings: 25,000 copies
Third printing (2018): 10,000 copies
Fourth printing (2020): 30,000 copies

books.bvks.com
books@bvks.com
Whatsapp # +(91) 7016811202

Published by Bhakti Vikas Trust, Surat
Printed in India

Dedication

Dedicated to Lord Śrī Kṛṣṇa Caitanya Mahāprabhu, to His foremost devotee in the modern age His Divine Grace A.C. Bhaktivedanta Swami Prabhupāda (founder-*ācārya* of the International Society for Krishna Consciousness), and to all preachers of Kṛṣṇa consciousness who dedicate their lives to bringing the mercy of Lord Caitanya to others.

śrī-kṛṣṇa-caitanya prabhu-nityānanda
śrī-advaita gadādhara śrīvāsādi-gaura-bhakta-vṛnda

I worship Lord Śrī Caitanya Mahāprabhu, whose nectarean mercy flows like a great river, inundating the entire universe. (*Caitanya-caritāmṛta*, *Ādi* 16.1)

Contents

Introduction

The Kṛṣṇa consciousness movement is now spread all over the world, yet its originator, Śrī Caitanya Mahāprabhu, remains largely unknown. Even in India, where at least the name of Lord Caitanya is widely familiar, most people know little about His activities or message. And even persons who know something of Lord Caitanya mostly misunderstand Him as merely a great devotee, whereas revealed scriptures uphold that He is the Supreme Personality of Godhead.

Drawing particularly from the voluminous original biographies *Śrī Caitanya-bhāgavata* and *Śrī Caitanya-caritāmṛta*, this introductory book attempts to summarize Lord Caitanya's activities and teachings. Certain customs, practices, and attitudes within traditional Hindu society as recounted herein, and even the very personage of Lord Caitanya, may seem strange to the unacquainted. Nonetheless, the reader is requested to give the text a patient and open-minded review, which will likely afford at least initial appreciation of Lord Caitanya's compassion and sweetness, and of His mood and mission. Detailed knowledge may be gathered by studying *Śrī Caitanya-caritāmṛta.** For the benefit of readers wholly new to this subject, a glossary and Sanskrit pronunciation guide are included at the back of this book.

* Available in English translation with extensive purports by His Divine Grace A.C. Bhaktivedanta Swami Prabhupāda, published by Bhaktivedanta Book Trust.

Prologue

Lord Caitanya has many names. His father titled Him Viśvambhara, and in His youth He was called Nimāi Paṇḍita. When He took *sannyāsa* He became Śrī Kṛṣṇa Caitanya. He was also renowned as Śrī Caitanya Mahāprabhu, or simply Mahāprabhu. And throughout His pastimes He was known as Gaurāṅga, or Gaurahari, because of His golden complexion.*

The Lord spent His first twenty-four years in Navadvīpa, West Bengal.† Thereafter He renounced family life and accepted *sannyāsa*. Making Purī His headquarters, Mahāprabhu then passed six years traveling between South India, Bengal, and Vṛndāvana. For the remaining eighteen years of His manifest presence He stayed in Purī, where He drifted into ever deeper trances of love for Kṛṣṇa.

The raptures exhibited by Lord Caitanya are unparalleled in the history of Eastern or Western religious mysticism. His biographers

---

* *Gaura*—golden or fair-complexioned.

† A town and area presently in the state of West Bengal, India.

have recorded that in the ecstasy of separation from Kṛṣṇa, sometimes Caitanya Mahāprabhu's head, arms, and legs would merge into His body in the manner of a tortoise, or His limbs become disjointed from His body and remain connected only by skin. Often when Mahāprabhu chanted Hare Kṛṣṇa and danced, His body would become covered with goose bumps, tears would squirt from His eyes as if from a syringe, and foam would ooze from His mouth. He would jump high into the air and crash down so heavily that the earth would shake. But due to spiritual rhapsody He would feel no pain and would continue to chant Hare Kṛṣṇa.

Gauḍīya Vaiṣṇava authorities acknowledge that such spiritual transformations are not possible for ordinary human beings, and thus identify Lord Caitanya as nondifferent from Lord Kṛṣṇa, the Supreme Personality of Godhead. Kṛṣṇa is famous as Śyāmasundara, or "He who is blackish and beautiful." And Lord Caitanya is Gaurasundara, "golden and beautiful," appearing in this wonderful fair feature due to combining with Rādhā, His eternal consort and pleasure potency. Thus Caitanya Mahāprabhu is the combined form of Rādhā and Kṛṣṇa but with the mood and complexion of Śrīmatī Rādhārāṇī, come to teach the world the worship of Śrī Śrī Rādhā-Kṛṣṇa.

As Lord Caitanya is glorious, so are His devotees. They are eternally liberated associates of Kṛṣṇa, descended to participate in the pastimes of His golden avatar. Biographers have recorded that Gaurāṅga's father, Jagannātha Miśra, is a combined avatar of Vasudeva and Nanda Mahārāja (respectively, the father and foster father of Kṛṣṇa in His Dvāpara-yuga *līlā*); His mother, Śacī, is a combined avatar of Devakī and Yaśodā (Kṛṣṇa's mother and foster mother, respectively); Nityānanda Prabhu is Balarāma, another form of the Supreme Personality of Godhead; Advaita Ācārya is a combined avatar of Mahāviṣṇu and Sadāśiva; Gadādhara Paṇḍita is Rādhārāṇī; Śrīvāsa Paṇḍita is Nārada Muni; Svarūpa Dāmodara is the *gopī* Viśākhā; and Rāmānanda Rāya is the *gopī* Lalitā.

Chapter One

Birth and Childhood Pastimes

Śrī Caitanya Mahāprabhu appeared in this world at a time of transformation in both the West and East. In Europe the Renaissance was flourishing, inspiring navigators to find new territories, astronomers to explore the heavens, and scholars to discover facts about the universe that overturned traditional paradigms and concepts. Simultaneously, in India a different kind of renaissance was taking place. Against a background of unprecedented social change, including widespread conversion of lower-class Hindus to Islam, the *bhakti* movement was revolutionizing religious outlooks and practices.

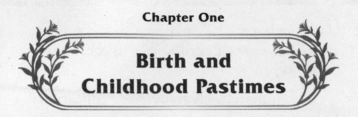

At that time many *brāhmaṇas* came to domicile in Navadvīpa, Bengal, being attracted by its location on the sacred Gaṅgā and its renown as a center of scholarship. One such *brāhmaṇa*, Jagannātha Miśra, migrated from East Bengal and settled on the bank of the Gaṅgā in Māyāpur, a neighborhood of Navadvīpa. Jagannātha Miśra was an exalted devotee of Lord Kṛṣṇa, as was his wife Śacīdevī.

Unfortunately, Navadvīpa's educational ambience was overwhelmingly materialistic, being based on mundane academics and sophistry. Navadvīpa's scholars and teachers prided themselves on their abilities in convoluted logic, semantic jugglery, and pedantic argumentation. Being content with formal observance of traditional rituals, most *brāhmaṇas* cared little for genuine religion and spurned authentic devotion to God, or Kṛṣṇa consciousness. Those few who taught *Bhagavad-gītā* spewed forth dry speculations instead of explaining its true devotional essence. And the religious aspirations of the unlettered masses went no further than worship of minor gods for procurement of worldly boons. Moreover, because Bengal was under Muslim rule and many Muslims lived in Navadvīpa, not only did Hindus live in constant fear of persecution, but they had to tolerate the sacrilege of cow slaughter being practiced openly in their midst.

Śrī Advaita Ācārya, the leader of Navadvīpa's small but dedicated Vaiṣṇava

Śrī Advaita Ācārya

community, worshiped Lord Kṛṣṇa with *tulasī* leaves and Gaṅgā water and beseeched Him to appear and rectify the situation. In answer to Advaita Ācārya's entreaties Lord Kṛṣṇa entered the womb of Śacīdevī, whose pregnancy endured for thirteen months. During this time Jagannātha Miśra would sometimes see divine beings in his home, yet he was unaware that they were demigods coming to pray to Lord Caitanya.

The Supreme Personality of Godhead, Śrī Caitanya Mahāprabhu, appeared in Māyāpur on the full-moon night of the month of Phālguna in the year 1407 Śakābda (18 February 1486 AD). Previously Śacīmātā had given birth to eight daughters, all of whom died immediately after birth. Thereafter she gave birth to a son, who survived and was named Viśvarūpa. Viśvambhara was to be her last child.

Śrī Caitanya Mahāprabhu appeared during an eclipse of the full moon. As per tradition, the Hindu residents of Navadvīpa stood within the Gaṅgā during the eclipse and chanted the divine names of Hari. Hearing them chant "Hari! Hari!" many Muslims mockingly imitated them. Thus, while the whole of Navadvīpa was vibrating the name of Śrī Hari, Gaurahari manifested Himself.

When Advaita Ācārya's wife, Śrīmatī Sītādevī, came to see the newborn baby, she discerned that this beautiful gold-colored boy had exactly the same features as Lord Śrī Kṛṣṇa and must indeed be Kṛṣṇa Himself, but with a different complexion. Because the child was born under a neem tree, and because most of Śacīmātā's other children had died prematurely, apparently due to the influence of evil spirits—against which the neem tree is reputed to be effective—for the infant's protection Sītādevī gave the name Nimāi.

Śrīmatī Sītādevī arrives

Lord Caitanya's maternal grandfather, Nīlāmbara Cakravartī, was a learned astrologer. On making Nimāi's chart he discovered that this child was the Supreme Personality of Godhead. But Nīlāmbara Cakravartī kept this confidential fact secret. He then met with other relatives and local scholars to choose a name for the baby. They declared, "As soon as this child was born, famine ended in the land, the farmers were blessed with rain, and the earth again became happy and prosperous, as if Lord Nārāyaṇa Himself were protecting the earth. Therefore this baby should be named Viśvambhara (maintainer of the worlds). After all, it is written in His horoscope that He will be a brilliant lamp shining in His family. 'Nimāi' may remain a secondary name."

During the name-giving ceremony, *brāhmaṇas* chanted auspicious mantras while local people were joined by disguised demigods in chanting the holy names of Lord Hari, blowing conchshells, and ringing bells. Various objects, such as rice grains, puffed rice, a book, coins, and gold and silver, were placed before the infant. Jagannātha Miśra said, "O my son Viśvambhara, please listen. Grasp whatever attracts Your mind." Ignoring everything else, the infant picked up the *Śrīmad-Bhāgavatam* and embraced it.

Everyone cheered and proclaimed, "He will be a distinguished *paṇḍita*."

Baby Nimāi would play a game with the doting neighborhood women who regularly came to see Him. He would start crying and would stop only when the ladies chanted "Hari! Hari!" In this way He induced them to chant all day long, and hence the home of Jagannātha Miśra continuously resounded with the names of Kṛṣṇa.

One day Śacīmātā and Jagannātha Miśra became aghast to see Nimāi playing in the courtyard with a big snake. They didn't know what to do, but after some time the serpent crawled around the body of the Lord and slithered away harmlessly. Actually the snake was Anantadeva, the resting place of Lord Viṣṇu.

Nimāi being kidnapped

Once two thieves entered the locality. Their specialty was kidnapping children and stealing their jewelry. Spotting Nimāi, they grabbed Him and ran off.

Unable to find her beloved Nimāi, distraught Śacīdevī called her neighbors to look for Him. Meanwhile, under the influence of the Lord's illusory potency, the befuddled crooks ran full-circle back to the house of Jagannātha Miśra. Seeing so many people looking for the child, they quickly put Nimāi down and fled.

As Nimāi grew up He became exceedingly mischievous, just as Kṛṣṇa had been in His childhood. One name of Kṛṣṇa is Duṣṭa Mohana, which means "naughty young boy." He is *duṣṭa* (naughty) yet His charming behavior enchants the mind (*mohana*). Nimāi also had this quality. His mother once found Him eating dirt. "Why are You eating dirt?" she asked. "I just gave You so many nice

Nimāi eats dirt

sweets." Nimāi replied, "What's the difference? It's all one. Sweets are produced from earth, so whether I eat sweets or dirt, it is the same." Being the wife of a learned Vaiṣṇava *brāhmaṇa*, Śacīmātā could understand that

Nimāi was expounding Advaita-vāda, the erroneous philosophy of absolute monism. She gave the example that although a clay pot is nothing but a transformation of earth, a lump of clay cannot be used as a pot; only when earth is transformed into a pot can it hold water. Similarly, even though sweets are produced from earth, she explained, crude earth cannot nourish the body as do sweets. Accepting the impracticality of monism, Viśvambhara proposed, "From now on give Me sweets and I will no longer eat dirt."

Seeing the full moon one evening Nimai called out, "Mother, Mother! Give Me the moon! Give it to Me!" And He began to cry. From within the house Śacīdevī brought a picture of Kṛṣṇa and presented it to her darling boy. When Gauracandra, the golden moon, saw Kṛṣṇacandra, the black moon, He became pacified.

When a certain *brāhmaṇa* on pilgrimage arrived at Navadvīpa, Jagannātha Miśra hosted him and supplied him rice and other provisions for his *śālagrāma-śilā*.* The *brāhmaṇa* cooked and offered everything, but

---

* From the river Gaṇḍakī, a genre of black stone that is nondifferent from Lord Viṣṇu and worshiped as such.

just then baby Nimāi came and ate some of the rice. Although the *brāhmaṇa* lamented that his offering had been defiled by restless Nimāi, upon Jagannātha Miśra's request he agreed to cook again. As the *brāhmaṇa* was offering the newly prepared items, again Nimāi came and tasted them. This time Jagannātha Miśra locked his son in a room, and after apologizing profusely, asked the *brāhmaṇa* to ready yet another meal. It was midnight and all were asleep when the pilgrim began to offer the food, but somehow baby Nimāi again arrived and ate it.

The *brāhmaṇa* was in tears. "Lord Viṣṇu does not want me to eat today," he thought. "I must have committed some offense." Then Nimāi said, "Don't you know that I am the same Lord Viṣṇu for whom you are daily preparing offerings?" He displayed His four-armed Viṣṇu form to the *brāhmaṇa*, who swooned in divine joy upon understanding that the child teasing him was none other than the Lord of his life.

Two *brāhmaṇa* devotees, Hiraṇya and Jagadīśa, lived in a distant neighborhood of Navadvīpa. Once on Ekādaśi they offered an elaborate *pūjā* to Lord Viṣṇu and prepared many delectable eatables for His pleasure. Somehow little Nimāi knew of this, and having walked from His home He demanded those palatable items. Hiraṇya and Jagadīśa were surprised at how the child could have known about this special offering, yet they happily gave Him the food.

Often at midday, when local *brāhmaṇas* would stand in the Gaṅgā to recite prayers and chant Gāyatrī, mischievous Nimāi would splash them, dive underwater and catch their legs to make them lose their balance, or spit on their bodies, forcing them to bathe repeatedly. He would throw sand on those who had just finished their bath and would mix up the men's and women's clothing on the riverbank, causing considerable embarrassment to all. Once when Nimāi understood that the *brāhmaṇas* were going to complain about Him to Jagannātha Miśra, He quickly jumped out of the water, got dressed, put ink on His fingers, and went home. When His father informed Him of the *brāhmaṇas'* grievances, He responded, "Father, I have just come from school! Just look at My fingers. I have not been to the Gaṅgā at all. They are making false accusations."

One time Nimāi playfully struck His mother. Pretending to faint, Śacīmātā fell down. The neighboring ladies told Nimāi, "Dear child, please bring a coconut from somewhere, then Your mother will be cured." Nimāi rushed out and immediately returned with two coconuts. Nobody knew how He could have got them so quickly.

The young girls of the area would assemble by the Gaṅgā and worship Lord Śiva, supplicating his benediction to get good husbands. Nimāi would sit among them and demand all the nice articles and food meant for Lord Śiva. He would tell them, "Worship Me, and I shall give you good husbands. Goddesses Gaṅgā and Durgā are My maidservants. What to speak of other demigods, even Lord Śiva is My servant." Nimāi warned the girls that if they did not comply He would curse them to get old husbands who already had several wives. In feigned anger the girls would scold Nimāi, but actually they relished His teasing them.

Nimāi demands offerings

While walking by the Gaṅgā one day, Nimāi saw a young maiden named Lakṣmīpriyā. She was actually an avatar of Lakṣmī. As Lakṣmī is the eternal consort of Kṛṣṇa, her expansion Lakṣmīpriyā is the eternal consort of Lord Caitanya, who is directly Kṛṣṇa. Upon seeing each other, the eternal affection between Lord Caitanya and Lakṣmīpriyā reawakened. She had brought garlands, sweets, and other paraphernalia for worshiping Lord Viṣṇu, but upon seeing Nimāi she immediately offered them to Him.

One day Śacīdevī found Nimāi atop a heap of discarded clay cooking pots and admonished Him for sitting in a contaminated place. Nimāi retorted with a complex explanation of the nature of purity and impurity: "Mother, that this is pure and that is impure is surely a worldly sentiment with no basis in fact. In these pots you have cooked food for Lord Viṣṇu and offered it to Him. How then can they be untouchable?

Nimāi discusses philosophy

Everything in relationship to Viṣṇu is to be considered an expansion of His energy. Being the Supersoul, Viṣṇu is eternal and uncontaminated. So why should these pots be regarded pure or impure?" Śacīdevī was surprised at her child's philosophical ability, but pragmatically had Him come down to bathe.

In a dream a divine being appeared to Jagannātha Miśra and reprimanded him for repeatedly rebuking Nimāi. Jagannātha Miśra explained that the boy was naughty. "If your child is already an elevated personality," the divine being reasoned, "then what will be the benefit in correcting Him? Better you desist." Jagannātha Miśra replied, "Even if my son is Lord Nārāyaṇa Himself, I am His father. It is my duty to discipline Him and I will continue to do so." Satisfied with Jagannātha Miśra's paternal resolve, the divine being disappeared.

Once Nimāi fell down at His mother's feet and begged her to give Him one thing. Śacīdevī replied, "My dear son, I will give You whatever You ask." Nimāi requested, "My dear Mother, please do not eat grains on Ekādaśi days." Mother Śacī agreed: "It is a good proposal. I shall not eat grains on Ekādaśi."

When Viśvarūpa heard that his parents were trying to arrange his marriage, he clandestinely left home and took *sannyāsa* with a vow never to return. Nimāi consoled His lamenting parents by assuring them that Viśvarūpa's renunciation was auspicious for the family, and by promising to remain at home to care for them in their old age.

When a beggar once came around, banging his drum and chanting the glories of Lord Śiva, young Nimāi assumed the form of Lord Śiva and danced on that devotee's shoulders.

In due course of time Jagannātha Miśra performed the sacred thread ceremony for Nimāi and sent Him to the school of Gaṅgādāsa Paṇḍita. Quickly mastering logic, grammar, and philosophy, Nimāi soon became noted as a competent scholar. Yet during this period He suffered the grief of His father's sudden passing away. Thereupon Śacīmātā, who was already much attached to Nimāi, her only son living at home, became wholly dependent on Him.

Chapter Two

The Adolescent Scholar

After the departure of Jagannātha Miśra, Nimāi's naughty behavior subsided. He became assiduous in following the duties prescribed for the brahminical order, such as regularly performing *sandhyā-vandanā*, and avoided the association of irreligious persons.* He opened a school for teaching Sanskrit and insisted that His students adhere to high standards. If any pupil came to school without *tilaka*, He would send him home, to return only after having applied it. Nimāi was diligent in study and never wasted time in idle gossip; nor would He ever look lustfully at or dally with women.

Nimāi took pleasure in debating with the many scholars of Navadvīpa, and was so incisive that others were afraid to meet Him. He would make a statement and ask the *paṇḍitas* to refute it. After they did, Nimāi would defeat their argument with another one

---

* *Sandhyā-vandanā*—prayers offered three times daily by *brāhmaṇas*.

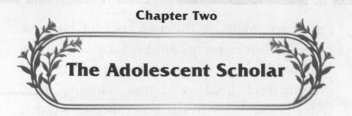

and then challenge them to counter His new position. But nobody could overcome Him, so He would rebut His own contention. He soon became renowned as "Nimāi Paṇḍita" and indeed behaved with the arrogance of a proud young *paṇḍita.*

A Vaiṣṇava of Navadvīpa named Śrīvāsa Paṇḍita once met Nimāi on the path to the Gaṅgā and petitioned, "My dear Nimāi, everything about You is laudable. You belong to a respectable *brāhmaṇa* family and excel in academics and religious duties. If You would only become a Vaiṣṇava then Your studies, aristocracy, and all else would be perfect. Don't You know that without worshiping Kṛṣṇa all learning is useless? The goal of scholarship is Kṛṣṇa. If You simply amass knowledge without dedicating Your life to Kṛṣṇa, You will become arrogant." Nimāi replied, "My dear Śrīvāsa, if I could get the blessings and association of pure devotees like yourself, then surely I could develop *kṛṣṇa-bhakti.*"

Nimāi delighted in inviting sannyasis and learned men to His home for *prasāda.* One such guest was Īśvara Purī, a sannyasi disciple of the exalted Vaiṣṇava renunciant Mādhavendra Purī. Īśvara Purī had written a book called *Śrī Kṛṣṇa-lilāmṛta,* which he showed to Nimāi. "Unlike You, I am not adept in Sanskrit, but I have drafted this manuscript. Please go through it and correct any errors." Nimāi replied, "My dear sir, you are a great devotee, so there can be no mistake in your expression. Even if superficially there is some flaw, your writing is perfect because it is inspired by Kṛṣṇa."

Nimāi used to stroll around the city and mingle with all kinds of people, irrespective of their caste or background. He would visit the homes of lepers, milkmen, merchants, garland makers, and others, charming everyone and endearing Himself to all by His sweet dealings. Wherever He went people offered Him gifts.

Upon once encountering an astrologer, Nimāi asked for information about His past life. The astrologer calculated, and then in meditation saw this beautiful young *brāhmaṇa* boy as the Absolute Truth, the source of all universes. Astonished, he reverentially addressed Nimāi, "You are the Supreme Personality of Godhead, the master and controller of all." Nimāi replied, "You are not a good astrologer.I happen to know that in My previous life I was a cowherd boy."

An elevated devotee named Śrīdhara lived in Navadvīpa. He supported himself by selling radishes, bananas, banana stalks, and banana-leaf cups. Despite his paltry income, half of whatever he earned he would use for worshiping Mother Gaṅgā. Every night he would loudly cry out "Hari! Nārāyaṇa!" Their sleep being disturbed, his neighbors would grumble, "Wretched Śrīdhara is calling out in distress because his stomach is empty and he cannot sleep."

Nimāi loved Śrīdhara very much but would repeatedly tease him. He would snatch vegetables from him and then offer a price far below their value.He once asked Śrīdhara, "Why are you worshiping Lakṣmī-Nārāyaṇa? What is the use of such adulation? They don't give you anything. You are such a poor man. You live in such a rundown house. Why don't you supplicate the demigods? They could help you."

Śrīdhara replied, "My dear Nimāi Paṇḍita, Time respects nobody. Whether one is rich or poor, animal or bird, Time keeps him engaged in reaping the results of his previous activities. Both men and animals enjoy life by eating, drinking, sleeping, and other sensual enjoyments, but Lord Śrī Hari can be worshiped only by human beings. So humans who do not worship Kṛṣṇa are no better than animals. That is why I don't care about my home or material condition. I worship Kṛṣṇa without desire for anything material."

Nimāi jokingly retorted, "You are a cheater. You have plenty of hidden treasure and are just pretending to be destitute. If you don't give Me a share of your riches I will expose you to others." "I am a poor man," Śrīdhara replied. "How can I offer You anything? You are a respectable *brāhmaṇa*. Why are You behaving like this?" But Nimāi would persist in His demands, and in the end Śrīdhara would give in: "Take any vegetable You want." So every day Nimāi would take freely from him.

"Who do you think I am?" Nimāi would ask Śrīdhara. "You are a young *brāhmaṇa* boy, part and parcel of Kṛṣṇa." "No, you are wrong. I am the maintainer of the Gaṅgā, who you worship." Unable to comprehend the truth of such words, Śrīdhara would cover his ears with his hands and shout, "Viṣṇu! Viṣṇu! What are You speaking? How can You claim to be God? Usually as people grow older they become wiser, but in You I find the opposite to be true." Śrīdhara could not recognize that the Lord of his heart had come to joke with him.

Nimāi married Lakṣmīpriyā, the same girl whom in childhood He had encountered on the bank of the Gaṅgā. As an ideal wife Lakṣmīpriyā faithfully performed her household duties and was always respectful toward Mother Śacī. Devoted to her husband, Lakṣmīpriyā cooked her Lord's meals and happily served His guests.

Every day Nimāi entertained many guests and also generously gave food and clothing to the poor. Śacīdevī worried, "How can we maintain such a lifestyle? We have no land or fixed income." Nimāi would assure her, "Mother, please do not fret. Lord Kṛṣṇa is the maintainer of the entire universe. If we depend on Him, surely He will manage everything for us." And it so happened that many unsolicited gifts kept coming to Nimāi's house.

Ostensibly to teach and thus earn some income for His household, Nimāi decided to go to East Bengal, although His undisclosed motive was to spread the chanting of the holy names in that province. During His sojourn in East Bengal many came to hear from this noted scholar of Navadvīpa. All became joyful by seeing His radiant golden form and hearing

His wonderful scriptural explanations. Whoever saw the Lord could not turn his eyes away from Him. The womenfolk would say, "I offer my respectful obeisances to the blessed woman who gave birth to such a son. And that fortunate and glorious lady who is His wife has certainly made her birth as a woman an outstanding success." Innumerable people offered abundant gifts to Nimāi—gold, silver, waterpots, sitting mats, rugs, and many varieties of clothing. Each happily presented the best of his possessions to the Lord.

In East Bengal lived a *brāhmaṇa* named Tapana Miśra. Eager to determine the meaning of life and how to attain it, he studied many books, but the more he read the more he became confused. One night in a dream a divine being directed him, "Miśra, why are you reading so many books? Nimāi Paṇḍita is nearby. He can answer all your questions and solve all your problems. Go visit Him." The next morning Tapana Miśra approached Nimāi and told Him of his situation.

Nimāi explained that the meaning of life cannot be ascertained by becoming a bookworm; in Kali-yuga one should simply chant the holy names of the Lord. As stated in *Bṛhan-nāradiya Purāṇa:*

harer nāma harer nāma harer nāmaiva kevalam
kalau nāsty eva nāsty eva nāsty eva gatir anyathā

"In this Age of Kali the only means of deliverance is to chant the holy names, chant the holy names, chant the holy names of Lord Śrī Hari. There is no other way, there is no other way, there is no other way."

Nimāi advised Tapana Miśra to constantly chant the *mahā-mantra*—Hare Kṛṣṇa, Hare Kṛṣṇa, Kṛṣṇa Kṛṣṇa, Hare Hare/ Hare Rāma, Hare Rāma, Rāma Rāma, Hare Hare—and assured him that thereby he could achieve all success. Tapana Miśra expressed a desire to renounce the world and follow Nimāi, but Nimāi directed him to settle in Varanasi, where they would meet in the future.

While Nimāi was in East Bengal, Lakṣmīpriyā's feelings of intense separation from Him assumed the form of a snake whose bite took her life. When Nimāi returned to Navadvīpa with much accumulated wealth, He consoled His mother, and on her request remarried. Nimāi's wedding festival was one of the greatest ever seen in Bengal. His new wife's name was Viṣṇupriyā.

Some time later an exceptional scholar from Kashmir, Keśava Kāśmīrī, visited Navadvīpa. He was a *digvijaya-paṇḍita* (one who has overcome all others in debate). Keśava Kāśmīrī would go from place to place challenging and defeating whoever dared to stand before him. Hearing of his arrival, all the savants of Navadvīpa fled, thus leaving young Nimāi as the only remaining *paṇḍita* in town.

One evening while wandering with His students on the bank of the Gaṅgā, Nimāi met Keśava Kāśmīrī. After offering respect, Nimāi asked him to demonstrate his scholarship by reciting some verses in praise of Mother Gaṅgā. Within half an hour Keśava Kāśmīrī composed one hundred verses. Nimāi then requested him to further demonstrate his skills by selecting any one of those verses

Hare Kṛṣṇa
Hare Kṛṣṇa
Kṛṣṇa Kṛṣṇa
Hare Hare
Hare Rāma
Hare Rāma
Rāma Rāma
Hare Hare

and analyzing its qualities and faults. Keśava Kāśmīrī asserted that the verses were flawless.

When Nimāi repeated one of the stanzas the *paṇḍita* became astonished: "How could You recall it? I uttered those verses like the blowing wind. How can You recall even one of them?" Nimāi replied, "As you are blessed by the goddess of learning Mother Sarasvatī, so am I. I am a *śruti-dhara* (one who perfectly remembers everything he hears)." Keśava Kāśmīrī proceeded to analyze the verse, pointing out the merits of the Sanskrit composition. "There is not even a trace of error in it," he concluded.

"If you do not mind," Nimāi suggested, "I could also say something about this stanza." Thinking that a young boy had no right to comment on the poetry of such a famous scholar as himself, the *digvijaya-paṇḍita* was reluctant to let Nimāi speak. Nimāi first described some merits which Keśava Kāśmīrī had not mentioned, but then exposed some serious defects in the oration. "Actually, it has unlimited faults," He averred. "I am merely pointing out the main ones."

The speechless *paṇḍita* returned to his residence and worshiped Sarasvatī, praying,

Sarasvatī appears in Kāśmīrī's dream

"Until now you have blessed me to conquer all other intellectuals, but today you have insulted me through the mouth of a young boy. What offense have I committed against you?"

That night Sarasvatī appeared to Keśava Kāśmīrī in a dream. "Keśava," she declared, "He who has defeated you is the object of my worship, the Supreme Personality of Godhead. You should surrender to Him." The next morning Keśava Kāśmīrī humbly approached Nimāi, who politely accepted the world-conquering scholar's submission. Nimāi's reputation in Navadvīpa was now unassailable.

Chapter Three

Initiation, and Starting the Saṅkīrtana Movement

In due course of time Nimāi went to Gayā with some of His students to perform the *śrāddha* ceremony for His departed father.*

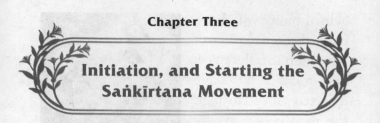

Viṣṇupāda Temple, Gaya

Upon taking *darśana* of the imprint of the lotus feet of Lord Viṣṇu, Nimāi became

* Gaya—a holy place in the present state of Bihar. Situated about 400 kilometers from Navadvīpa, it is famous for its temple of Lord Viṣṇu's lotus feet, in which place *śrāddha* (rites for deceased relatives) is especially effective.

overwhelmed with transcendental joy. Īśvara Purī, whom Nimāi had once entertained in Navadvīpa, happened to be in Gayā. They greeted and embraced each other with tears of delight. Nimāi submitted, "My pilgrimage to Gayā has become successful upon gaining the *darśana* of a saintly personality like you. Actually, your lotus feet are themselves the abode of all holy places. Therefore I require to take shelter of and dedicate My life to them." Hence Īśvara Purī initiated Nimāi Paṇḍita and instructed Him to constantly chant the names of Kṛṣṇa. He also warned Nimāi, "You think You are a great *paṇḍita*, but actually You are not qualified to study Vedānta."

Lord Caitanya is the Supreme Personality of Godhead, the object and source of all knowledge. Even from the external point of view He was a great scholar. Yet He accepted a guru to demonstrate to all other persons the absolute necessity of doing so. Similarly, by scolding Lord Caitanya, Īśvara Purī showed that however capable a disciple may be, he should be ready to accept correction from his guru. Īśvara Purī's words to the Lord "You are a fool and are not fit to study Vedānta" are particularly relevant for people in the modern age, practically all of whom are unqualified to enter into the complexities of Vedic philosophy, and hence for whom chanting the holy names of Kṛṣṇa is the only recommended process. Therefore Īśvara Purī told Lord Caitanya to chant those holy names incessantly.

Soon thereafter Viśvambhara returned to question Īśvara Purī, "My dear lord, what kind of mantra have you given Me? It has made me mad. While chanting Hare Kṛṣṇa, sometimes I dance, sometimes cry, and sometimes fall to the ground." Īśvara Purī laughed in joy and replied, "My dear boy, it is good that by chanting Hare Kṛṣṇa You have achieved the perfection of life. The very nature of the Hare Kṛṣṇa *mahā-mantra* is to increase attachment to Kṛṣṇa. Go on chanting and induce others to chant, and in this way save the entire world by spreading the *saṅkīrtana* movement."

Thereupon Viśvambhara gave up His pride of scholarship and became completely intoxicated with love for Kṛṣṇa. On the way back to Navadvīpa He continuously chanted Hare Kṛṣṇa in ecstasy. With difficulty His students helped Him complete the journey, for He kept swooning in love of Kṛṣṇa.

Viśvambhara performs kīrtana

Nimāi arrived home as if a different person, sometimes shedding tears in separation from Kṛṣṇa, the Lord of His heart, and at other times singing the names of Kṛṣṇa or talking animatedly of Kṛṣṇa's charms, attributes, and pastimes. The Vaiṣṇavas of Navadvīpa exulted in the transformation of Nimāi from an arrogant young scholar to a God-intoxicated devotee.

At His Sanskrit school Lord Viśvambhara now explained every word and syllable to mean Kṛṣṇa. Thus His pupils submitted, "Your system of education has changed. What You are teaching is not accepted by other scholars. How shall we learn anything?" Nimāi replied, "Forgive Me, but I can no longer explain anything except Kṛṣṇa, His names, and His pastimes. I give you complete freedom to study under anyone else, because in this condition it will be impossible for Me to teach you." The students responded, "Then we shall also give up academics, for where can we find another instructor like You? Birth after birth we desire to treasure in our hearts the explanations we have heard from You. What is the use of further study? To whom could we go? All that we have learned from You is more than sufficient for us."

Nimāi spent His days talking with the Vaiṣṇavas of Navadvīpa about Kṛṣṇa, and His nights chanting Hare Kṛṣṇa with them. To experience the joy of serving His own devotees and to set an example for the general populace, Gaurāṅga started assisting the Vaiṣṇavas. He would carry their clothes, *pūjā* items, sandalwood paste, and flower baskets when they would go to worship and bathe in the Gaṅgā. He thereby demonstrated how Vaiṣṇavas should be tended, even though He Himself is the ultimate object of service for all devotees.

Śacīdevī grew apprehensive—had her son become mad? And would His new beatitude lead Him to embrace the path of renunciation as had His brother? She asked Him, "Why do You now always chant the name of Kṛṣṇa?" Gaurāṅga explained, "All the scriptures point toward Kṛṣṇa. The holy names, qualities, and pastimes of Kṛṣṇa are the only eternal truths of the scriptures. Other writings have no absolute value. Only scriptures that describe Kṛṣṇa are to be relied upon and regarded as sacred." Nimāi asked Śacīdevī to take up Kṛṣṇa consciousness in full sincerity and enthusiasm. She agreed, and also became merged in the nectar of pure devotional service.

Gaurāṅga was becoming more and more intoxicated in love of Kṛṣṇa. Without caring for others' opinions, He would sing, dance, laugh, and weep like a madman. Unable to understand His behavior, Śacīdevī asked her neighbors for advice. They deemed Nimāi an epileptic, so recommended that she apply ointment to His head. Ignoring their counsel, Śacīdevī prayed to the family deity Govinda for help. And she called Śrīvāsa Paṇḍita, whom she much respected, to help her find a cure. When Gaurāṅga saw the revered devotee Śrīvāsa Paṇḍita in His

Gaurāṅga intoxicated in love of Kṛṣṇa

house, His transcendental madness only increased. Śrīvāsa assured Śacīdevī, "There is no cause for worry. Rather, you should be happy, for your son is exhibiting the symptoms of an exalted devotee of Kṛṣṇa."

One day Gaurāṅga asked His intimate friend Gadādhara Paṇḍita, "Where is Kṛṣṇa? Please tell Me where Kṛṣṇa is!" Gadādhara replied, "Kṛṣṇa is within Your heart." Nimāi then started to tear His skin to extract Kṛṣṇa from His heart. "Don't worry! Don't worry!" Gadādhara consoled Him. "Kṛṣṇa will come very soon." Seeing Nimāi thus pacified, Śacīdevī requested Gadādhara to always remain with her unpredictable son to protect Him.

Observing some cows grazing on the bank of the Gaṅgā one day, Gaurāṅga remembered His previous *līlā* in Vṛndāvana and called out, "I am He! I am He!" He ran to the house of Śrīvāsa Paṇḍita, who was worshiping his deity of Lord Nṛsiṁhadeva. "O Śrīvāsa," He exclaimed, "Behold Him whom you worship, now present before you!" Śrīvāsa opened his eyes and saw Gaurāṅga in a four-armed form, holding a conch, disc, club, and lotus flower.* Overwhelmed, Śrīvāsa Paṇḍita wept with delight. Gaurāṅga then asked Śrīvāsa to worship Him with the paraphernalia he had prepared for Nṛsiṁhadeva. Having done this, Śrīvāsa and his family bowed down before the Lord, who being pleased, put His lotus feet on their heads.

Thereupon Lord Gaurāṅga showed to Śrīvāsa His form as Kṛṣṇa and assured him, "Do not be afraid of anyone opposing the *saṅkīrtana* movement. Since I am in everyone's heart, no one can do anything against My will. I can inspire even wild jungle animals with *kṛṣṇa-prema.*" To prove His abilities He called Nārāyaṇī, Śrīvāsa's four-year-old niece, and ordered her, "Nārāyaṇī, chant Hare Kṛṣṇa and cry in ecstasy." Immediately Nārāyaṇī began dancing and weeping, intoxicated in rapturous divine love. Thenceforth Śrīvāsa Paṇḍita and family became staunch followers of Lord Caitanya. At home they would regularly perform *saṅkīrtana* all night long.

Nityānanda Prabhu had appeared in another part of Bengal. When He was just a

* These items are generally held in the four hands of Lord Nārāyaṇa, of whom Nṛsiṁhadeva is an expansion.

Nityānanda Prabhu

young boy, a wandering sannyasi had come to His parents' abode and taken Him away with their permission. Since then He had been traveling all over India. While in Mathurā He had heard about Gaurāṅga, so He came to Navadvīpa, where He stayed incognito in the house of the devotee Nandana Ācārya. Knowing that Nityānanda had arrived, Gaurāṅga sent Haridāsa Ṭhākura and Śrīvāsa Paṇḍita to find Him. They searched all throughout the town but returned unsuccessful, upon which the all-knowing Gaurāṅga Himself proceeded to the house of Nandana Ācārya. Seeing Lord Nityānanda dancing and crying with blissful love for Kṛṣṇa, Lord Caitanya and the accompanying Vaiṣṇavas wept. When Nimāi embraced Him, Nityānanda became still.

Now estranged from the wrangling scholars, Gaurāṅga was spearheading a Vaiṣṇava revival in Navadvīpa. Nityānanda

Prabhu became His main assistant, and Śrīvāsa Paṇḍita's house His headquarters.

On Guru-pūrṇimā, the annual festival when one's guru is worshiped along with the original guru Vyāsadeva, Lord Caitanya requested Nityānanda Prabhu to offer homage to Vyāsadeva in a ceremony at Śrīvāsa Paṇḍita's house. Nityānanda Prabhu was supposed to offer a garland to Vyāsadeva, but instead placed it on Gaurāṅga's shoulders, understanding Him to be the personality from whom everything emanates and whose empowered avatar is Śrī Vyāsadeva. Thereupon Lord Caitanya manifested a six-armed form, holding in four hands Lord Viṣṇu's conch, disc, club, and lotus, respectively, and in the other two, Lord Balarāma's plough and club.

Another day at Śrīvāsa's house, Gaurāṅga sat in the place reserved for worship of Viṣṇu and remained there for twenty-one hours while His devotees worshiped Him with flowers, *tulasī* leaves, Gaṅgā water, sweets, and other suitable offerings. The great Vaiṣṇava *ācārya* Bhaktivinoda Ṭhākura envisioned this scene and described it in a song:

śrī-kṛṣṇa-caitanya prabhu-nityānanda
śrī-advaita gadādhara śrīvāsādi-gaura-bhakta-vṛnda

All glories, all glories to the beautiful *ārati* ceremony of Lord Śrī Kṛṣṇa Caitanya Mahāprabhu, who is like a golden moon. That *ārati* ceremony takes place on the banks of the Jāhnavī (Gaṅgā) in Navadvīpa and attracts the minds of all people in the universe. Lord Caitanya sits on a jeweled throne. To His right stands Lord Nityānanda, and on His left is Śrī Gadādhara. Nearby stands Śrī Advaita Ācārya, and Śrīvāsa Paṇḍita is holding a royal umbrella over the Lord's head. Lord Brahmā, assisted by all the demigods, performs the *ārati*. The intimate

> associate Narahari leads others in waving yak-tail whisks, while the brothers Sanjay, Mukunda, and Basu Ghosh sing sweetly. Conches blow, bells ring, *karatālas* chime, and *mṛdaṅgas* resound sweetly. Lord Caitanya's face shines more brilliantly than millions of moons. His neck is adorned with an effulgent garland of forest flowers. With voices choked in the ecstasy of love for God, Lord Śiva, Nārada Muni, and Śukadeva Gosvāmī proclaim the glories of Gaurāṅga.

One of Śrīvāsa's housemaids, named Duḥkhī, tirelessly brought water from the Gaṅgā for ceremonially bathing the Lord. Seeing her devotion Gaurāṅga changed her name to Sukhī.* The devotees then began singing hymns praising Lord Caitanya's avatars in the different ages. The Lord manifested to the devotees His magnificent glory, power, beauty, and opulence and then assumed forms of His different avatars, revealing Himself as Kṛṣṇa, Nārāyaṇa, Rāma, and others. Each devotee saw Gaurāṅga in the aspect he was most attached to

* *Duḥkhī*—unhappy; *sukhī*—happy.

worshiping. Then the Lord called all the devotees individually and disclosed secrets about their lives—how they had begun to worship the Lord, how He had saved them in difficulty, and so on. In this way Gaurāṅga demonstrated that He knew the heart of every devotee and was protecting them.

Previously Śrīdhara had admonished Gaurāṅga for calling Himself Viṣṇu, but now he was delighted to see that Gaurāṅga was actually Lord Viṣṇu. Yet when Gaurāṅga offered him whatever riches he wanted, Śrīdhara declared, "My dear Lord, I don't want any material benediction from You. I desire only this boon: wherever and whenever I may be born, You will be my master birth after birth." Lord Caitanya was pleased to fulfil Śrīdhara's desire.

Noticing that the Lord had not called His childhood friend Mukunda Datta, the devotees inquired why. Gaurāṅga replied, "Mukunda mixes with Māyāvādīs, those rascals who maintain that the absolute truth is without form, name, attributes, or qualities. Don't let him come." Hearing this from outside, Mukunda became brokenhearted. Through the devotees he asked Lord Caitanya when he would again be able to approach Him. The Lord replied, "After ten million births." When this was conveyed to Mukunda, he danced with glee. "I may have to wait ten million births," he thought, "but finally I will see my Lord again." When Gaurāṅga heard of Mukunda's eagerness to wait so patiently for His *darśana*, He immediately sent for him. Warning him to never again mix with persons envious of Kṛṣṇa, the Lord forgave his offenses.

Viśvambhara was daily holding all-night *kīrtanas* at Śrīvāsa's house, but nondevotees were not allowed inside. Even Śrīvāsa's mother-in-law could not enter, because of her anti-devotional attitude. Finding the door shut for them, malicious men cast aspersions on the spotless character of the Lord's devotees, who nevertheless cared not for such envious persons.

Kīrtana at Śrīvāsa's house

Upon being refused admittance, a scoundrel *brāhmaṇa* named Gopāla Cāpāla retaliated by placing outside the gate of Śrīvāsa Paṇḍita's house wine, flesh, and other paraphernalia for worshiping the goddess Durgā, as if to prove that Śrīvāsa was actually a degraded worshiper of Durgā and merely posing as a Vaiṣṇava. For this offense Gopāla Cāpāla was attacked with leprosy and suffered for many months, until Lord Caitanya eventually delivered him.

Another foul-mouthed *brāhmaṇa* who was denied entry snapped his sacred thread in a fit of rage and cursed Gaurāṅga, "Let Your worldly happiness come to an end!" Gaurāṅga happily accepted the supposed malediction, thus showing that for a person serious about developing Kṛṣṇa consciousness, complete destruction of prosperity and worldly desires is a sign of God's grace.

A *brahmacārī* who subsisted only on milk begged Śrīvāsa Paṇḍita to allow him in to see the *kīrtana*. But Gaurāṅga rejected him as an outsider and mere sightseer. "Performance of any amount of severe austerities or renunciation does not please Me," He declared. "I am satisfied only by unadulterated devotion." The *brahmacārī* accepted the reprimand in good faith and surrendered to the Lord's lotus feet.

One evening when Gaurāṅga and His devotees were blissfully chanting and dancing, a son of Śrīvāsa Paṇḍita's died. Yet Śrīvāsa prohibited his family members from weeping, lest they disturb the Lord's ecstasy. Late into the night Gaurāṅga heard of the mishap and immediately went with His associates to see the dead child. The departed soul then reentered the body and explained the mystery of his sudden departure: "I am a *jīva* (soul). By the will of the Lord I came here through my parents Śrīvāsa Paṇḍita and Mālinī Devī. And also by the will of the Lord my life span ended. Now I am departing to another existence. O Lord, please bless me to be Your eternal servitor wherever I am born. I offer my humble obeisances at Your lotus feet and the lotus feet of Your associates. Please be merciful unto me." The soul then left his body amid loud chanting of the holy names, and Śrīvāsa's family members were relieved of their grief.

The indigent devotee Śuklāmbara Brahmacārī, undisturbed by his poverty, lived an exemplary life of service to the Supreme

Lord. One day while returning to his hut after soliciting alms, he met Gaurāṅga, who forcibly took some grains of rice from his begging bag and ate them. The Lord did this to confirm the scriptural truth that He accepts with tremendous relish even an insignificant morsel offered with loving devotion, but does not care for opulent dishes offered by rich atheists.

If Viśvambhara heard someone singing the glories of Kṛṣṇa, He would immediately become enraptured. Crying out "Kṛṣṇa!" in response, He would tremble in delight and become covered in goose bumps, His hairs standing erect. Similarly, while chanting and dancing He often became oblivious to all else—He might collapse on the ground and remain there for hours with unceasing rivers of tears gushing from His eyes. Sometimes during the day the Lord would ask what time of night it was. Totally absorbed in love of God, Gaurāṅga simply cried and cried.

When in external consciousness, Viśvambhara would cordially converse with His followers and admirers, and would also give charity, perform formal worship in His home, and respectfully dine on *prasāda*. Thus

He joyfully passed His days and nights steeped in transcendental love of Kṛṣṇa.

Once when Gaurāṅga was narrating the glories of the holy name to His devotees, a student from outside His group tauntingly remarked, "To state that salvation is possible only by the Lord's name, to the exclusion of other religious practices, is an exaggeration. Such dogmatism should find no favor among learned *paṇḍitas*." Lord Caitanya exclaimed, "To consider the glories of the holy name as eulogistic or merely exaggeration is a severe offense." He quoted from scripture: "In Kali-yuga the Supreme Lord Kṛṣṇa has revealed Himself in the form of His holy names, the chanting of which is the only panacea for all miseries. Persons who resort to processes other than chanting Hare Kṛṣṇa are doomed to destruction." Viśvambhara further stated that a devotee who aspires to chant the holy name purely must practice being humbler than a blade of grass and more tolerant than a tree; despite provocation, he must not give way to lust and anger. He should respect others yet not desire honor for himself.

Lord Gaurāṅga directed Nityānanda and Haridāsa to go door to door in Navadvīpa and entreat everyone to worship Kṛṣṇa, chant His holy names, and study His teachings. Once while preaching they came across Jagāi and Mādhāi, two brothers infamous as drunkards, meat-eaters, and the worst of violent criminals. Being an ocean of transcendental compassion, Lord Nityānanda desired to deliver these rogues and thus requested them to chant the names of Kṛṣṇa. In response, Mādhāi threw at Nityānanda Prabhu a piece of earthen pot, which struck Him on the head and drew blood. Thereupon Jagāi tried to restrain Mādhāi.

Hearing news of this attack on Lord Nityānanda, who was dearer to Him than His own life, the incensed Gaurāṅga rushed to the spot and called for His eternal disc weapon, Sudarśana, to kill Jagāi and Mādhāi. Seeing the Lord's fury, Jagāi repented and begged forgiveness. But Mādhāi did not, so Nityānanda had to restrain Lord Caitanya. "My dear Lord, please don't kill him," He implored. "We have come to this world to save all fallen, wretched, pathetic sinners. We should uplift Jagāi and Mādhāi. Then We will protect Our reputation as the purifiers of the fallen (*patita-pāvana*). In other ages We killed many demons. Let Us now deliver these two wrongdoers."

Deliverance of Jagāi and Mādhāi

Gaurāṅga then forgave Jagāi and Mādhāi on the condition that they forever cease sinning and always chant the holy names of the Lord. Henceforward these former terrors of Navadvīpa became famous as exalted devotees, which caused the glories of Lord Caitanya to spread even more. In this pastime Māhaprabhu demonstrated that although a devotee should be humble and forbearing and should forgive infringements toward himself, he must not tolerate any offense against Kṛṣṇa or His devotee—rather, he should become angry.

One day after performing *saṅkīrtana*, the Lord and His devotees sat down to rest. Gaurāṅga planted a mango seed, which immediately grew into a tree laden with fruit. Every day for one year the devotees enjoyed fruit from this magical mango tree.

Another evening, the devotees were about to start *saṅkīrtana* when suddenly thunder, lightning, and heavy clouds signaled the onset of a storm. Lord Gaurāṅga then took *karatālas* in His hands and began chanting the Hare Kṛṣṇa *mahā-mantra*, looking up toward the sky as if to direct the demigods in the higher planets. Seeing the clouds disperse as quickly as they had assembled, the devotees chanted, danced, and jumped with joy.

Evening kīrtana

In her home Śacīdevī used to worship deities of Kṛṣṇa and Balarāma. One night she dreamt that Nimāi and Nitāi (Gaurāṅga and Nityānanda) had come to take the offering she had cooked for Kṛṣṇa and Balarāma, who then protested, "What are You doing? This is Our offering!" Nimāi and Nitāi were replying, "No, no. In Kali-yuga We are Kṛṣṇa and Balarāma, so We are taking the food." The next day while serving *prasāda* to Nimāi and Nitāi, Śacīdevī saw Them transformed into Kṛṣṇa and Balarāma as young boys, happily accepting her offering. Mother Śacī wept and then fainted in joy.

When one day Gaurāṅga started calling out "Puṇḍarīka! Puṇḍarīka!" His devotees wondered to whom the Lord was referring. Gaurāṅga explained that His intimate devotee Puṇḍarīka Vidyānidhi, from Chattagram in East Bengal, would soon visit Navadvīpa. Since Mukunda Datta was also originally from Chattagram, he was well aware of Puṇḍarīka Vidyānidhi's exalted qualities. After Puṇḍarīka Vidyānidhi came to Navadvīpa, Mukunda asked Gadādhara Paṇḍita if he would like to visit a Vaiṣṇava, and Gadādhara affirmed that he was always eager to meet Vaiṣṇavas.

Arriving at the house of Puṇḍarīka Vidyānidhi, they found him being fanned by servants while he sat on a large white bedstead. He was adorned in fine silk, his long curly hair was scented with fragrant oil, and now and then he would spit pan into a silver spittoon. Young Gadādhara, a strict *brahmacārī*, became doubtful. "This person doesn't look like a Vaiṣṇava," he thought. "He seems to be a worldly enjoyer." Understanding Gadādhara's mind, Mukunda sang a verse from *Śrīmad-Bhāgavatam* describing the glories of Śrī Kṛṣṇa, thus causing Puṇḍarīka Vidyānidhi to become wild in ecstatic love. He fell off his seat, his flailing arms and legs smashing everything in sight. Then for several hours he ran hither and thither, crying out "Kṛṣṇa! Kṛṣṇa!" No one could restrain him.

Gadādhara mused, "I failed to recognize this devotee's elevated status. I committed an offense by considering him an ordinary materialist. How can I atone for this? Although acceptance of a spiritual master is essential for spiritual progress, I have not yet been formally initiated. I will offer my life to Puṇḍarīka Vidyānidhi and request him to make me his disciple." When Puṇḍarīka eventually returned to external consciousness, Mukunda submitted to him Gadādhara's plea, to which Puṇḍarīka acquiesced, declaring himself fortunate to attain such a qualified disciple.

Devānanda Paṇḍita, a learned *brāhmaṇa* living in Navadvīpa, used to lecture daily on *Śrīmad-Bhāgavatam* to a large audience. When Śrīvāsa Paṇḍita once attended Devānanda's discourse, he became overwhelmed with *kṛṣṇa-prema* and wept loudly. Not appreciating Śrīvāsa's transcendental position, Devānanda's students removed Śrīvāsa from the assembly as Devānanda watched silently without restraining them. Being a Māyāvādī, Devānanda could not understand the essence of *Śrīmad-Bhāgavatam* and failed to comprehend that the devotee *Bhāgavata* and book *Bhāgavata* are equally sacred. Thus through his disciples he committed a serious offense against Śrīvāsa.

Some days later, when Caitanya Mahāprabhu happened to pass by Devānanda's house, He severely deprecated him for his Māyāvāda interpretation of *Śrīmad-Bhāgavatam*. Devānanda had little faith in Śrī Caitanya Mahāprabhu or in the path of pure devotional service, but when after some time he heard the great devotee Vakreśvara Paṇḍita explain the science of Kṛṣṇa, his mind changed and he was induced to explain *Śrīmad-Bhāgavatam* according to Vaiṣṇava understanding.

Viśvambhara's spiritual revival was shaking Navadvīpa's Hindu residents out of their materialistic stupor. Throughout the town, small groups of people would gather in their homes to chant the holy names. Thus Gaurāṅga was considered a threat by orthodox *brāhmaṇas* of Navadvīpa, according to whom He had previously been a good young man, but since returning from Gayā had become crazy and was disrupting the Hindu religion. "How could anyone go into the streets and chant the names of God with all different castes of people?" they protested. "Surely this will spoil all religious customs!"

The *brāhmaṇas* complained to the Kazi, the Muslim magistrate in charge of the area, who then ordered that the *saṅkīrtana* be stopped. He personally entered a house from which the strains of *kīrtana* were emanating, broke a *mṛdaṅga*, and warned the indwellers of the dire consequences they could expect if they did not forswear chanting. Seeing His followers downcast, Nimāi assured them, "Do not be afraid. This evening we will bring out a huge *saṅkīrtana* party. Let's see what kind of Kazi will try to stop us." Accordingly, Gaurāṅga led a massive procession through the streets and alleyways of Navadvīpa and along the bank of the Gaṅgā to the Kazi's home. Some of Nimāi's followers began destroying the house and garden, but Nimāi restrained them and sent for the Kazi.

After pacifying the Kazi and explaining that He had not come with malicious intent, Nimāi discussed with him at length. He spoke on the basis of Vedic scriptures, while the Kazi represented the Koran. Ultimately the Kazi admitted that cow slaughter was against the true principles of religion and promised Gaurāṅga, "Neither I nor any of my

Discussion with the Kazi on the basis of Vedic scriptures

descendants will ever hinder Your *saṅkīrtana* movement." And he also joined the *saṅkīrtana* parade through the streets of Navadvīpa.

One time while roaming the countryside, Lord Caitanya visited the home of some cowherds and ate some milk sweets there. As He walked toward a nearby pond, the cowherd men warned Him that a dangerous crocodile lived therein. But Gaurāṅga was undaunted. Espying the crocodile, He stretched out His beautiful lotus foot and placed it on the beast's head. Immediately the crocodile assumed an effulgent divine form and explained, "In my previous life I was a mischievous young boy. Once I pulled the legs of a sage who was standing in the water chanting Gāyatrī and he then cursed me to become a crocodile. When I prayed for forgiveness he replied, 'Don't worry. Soon Lord Kṛṣṇa will appear here as Gaurāṅga and deliver you by the touch of His lotus feet.'"

Sometimes before sunrise Gaurāṅga would take His devotees in a *saṅkīrtana* procession through the neighboring towns and villages. To the sound of *mṛdaṅgas* and *karatālas,* He would dance along the path, His body trembling in rapture and the ankle bells on

His feet chiming sweetly. The devotees would loudly call out Kṛṣṇa's names—Mukunda! Mādhava! Yādava! Hari!—and request the townsfolk to do likewise.

Saṅkīrtana procession before sunrise

"Why do you uselessly waste your lives simply caring for your bodies?" they would ask them. "Don't you know what a rare gift this human form of life affords? If you do not worship Lord Kṛṣṇa, the darling of Mother Yaśodā, then you will fall into the darkest ignorance. Now that the sun is rising you are preparing for another busy day, yet you fail to consider how each rising and setting of the sun reduces your life. Why do you not care to worship Śrī Kṛṣṇa, the Lord of your heart?

This life is temporary and full of miseries and dangers. Therefore while going on with your daily activities, take shelter of the holy name of Kṛṣṇa. The all-attractive name of Kṛṣṇa has arisen to bless the living entities. Take shelter of this holy name, the essence of all nectar. In all the fourteen worlds there is nothing to be gained but the name."

A Muslim tailor who lived near Śrīvāsa Paṇḍita's home used to sew garments for Śrīvāsa's family. One day he was fortunate enough to see Caitanya Mahāprabhu's dancing, and became enchanted. Appreciating the tailor's devotional attitude, the Lord showed His original form as Kṛṣṇa, whereupon the tailor began to dance and exclaim, "I have seen! I have seen!" Absorbed in ecstatic love, he then danced with Mahāprabhu. Thenceforth he became one of the principle devotees of Lord Caitanya.

Innumerable people, including many demigods and residents of other planets, would come to visit Gaurāṅga in His home. The Lord would receive them courteously, and in a sweet voice advise them, "Simply worship Kṛṣṇa and chant and sing His divine names.

No one should think of anything but Kṛṣṇa. If you actually have affection for Me, then do not discuss any topic but Kṛṣṇa. Whether eating, sleeping, or remaining awake, in all circumstances and throughout the day and night, always think only of Kṛṣṇa and utter His names."

One day Nimāi was sitting at home chanting "*Gopī, gopī, gopī*," meditating on the qualities of the *gopīs* and immersed in the mood of loving anger that the *gopīs* sometimes feel toward Kṛṣṇa. A visiting student challenged, "Why are You chanting '*gopī*'? Why don't You chant the name of Kṛṣṇa?" Overwhelmed by the self-righteousness of a *gopī* in an amorous quarrel with Kṛṣṇa, Gaurāṅga grabbed a stick and chased the student, shouting, "Don't say the name of Kṛṣṇa! We have nothing to do with Kṛṣṇa!" When the fleeing student reached his friends he told them, "Nimāi Paṇḍita has become too proud. I'm from a respectable *brāhmaṇa* family and was giving Him good advice, yet He wanted to strike me." The students then decided that should Nimāi ever repeat such behavior, they would conjointly beat Him to teach Him a lesson.

When Nimāi returned to normal consciousness He reflected that, apart from His intimate devotees, most people considered Him an ordinary person and did not understand His mission—to deliver everyone in the world by spreading the chanting of Hare Kṛṣṇa. Lord Caitanya considered, "If I accept *sannyāsa*, people will take My teachings seriously. Following the etiquette of offering obeisances to a sannyasi, they will at least bow down before Me. Since I am the Supreme Personality of Godhead, they will be benefited by prostrating before Me. And by taking *sannyāsa* I will be relieved of family responsibilities and be free to travel and preach." Thus the Lord resolved to save the entire world by adopting *sannyāsa*.

Chapter Four

Acceptance of Sannyāsa and Arrival in Purī

The devotees were thunderstruck at the prospect of losing their Nimāi. Especially His mother was most distraught at the thought of separation from her darling son. But Lord Gaurāṅga consoled her, "Mother, do not be affected by meaningless miseries or subject to covetousness, anger, false pride, or illusion. Please consider who you really are, who your son is, and who your father is. Why lament over false designations of "yours" and "mine"? Who is a woman? Who is one's husband? The only real shelter is Kṛṣṇa's lotus feet. Kṛṣṇa is the only father and only friend. Kṛṣṇa is the Absolute Lord. He is the supreme treasure. Without Kṛṣṇa everything is useless.

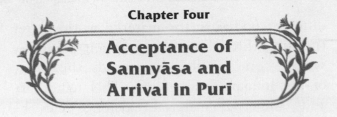

"Being bound by the Lord's illusory energy, the whole world is controlled like a machine. Due to pride and false ego everyone suffers. One who considers the consequences of his actions will decide to act in a pious manner. Still, his karmic reactions will bind him in the next life. Forgetting Kṛṣṇa, such a fool takes different bodies in the material world. After traveling throughout the fourteen planetary systems, one finally understands the rarity of the human form of life. This temporary and dangerous material existence can be extinguished in a moment. Appreciating the rarity of human birth, one should serve Kṛṣṇa and become free from illusion. These bodies are meant only for serving Kṛṣṇa, and by doing so one attains salvation. Simply by loving Kṛṣṇa you will become free from the cycle of birth and death. Mother, had you offered your affection to Kṛṣṇa instead of Me, you would have benefited immensely.

"Kṛṣṇa is the real friend and well-wisher. And the real mother and father are they who give their offspring pure love for the lotus feet of Kṛṣṇa. My heart cries in separation from Kṛṣṇa. Falling at your feet, I am praying to you. Mother, you have been so loving to Me throughout My whole life. My liberation will guarantee your liberation also. Please give up your attachment to Me and serve the lotus feet of Kṛṣṇa.

"I must take *sannyāsa* to attain love of Kṛṣṇa. Then I will take the treasure of *kṛṣṇa-prema* to different countries. Other mothers' sons bring the transient treasures of gold and silver, which simply cause misery and death. Enjoying wealth and opulence is not the goal of life. Love of Kṛṣṇa is eternal and imperishable in this world and the next. In every life one gets a father and mother, but rarely does one obtain a spiritual master and Kṛṣṇa. In the human form of life one should understand the importance of serving guru and Kṛṣṇa. One who does not accept a spiritual master is no better than a bird or beast."

Shortly thereafter a sannyasi named Keśava Bhāratī visited Navadvīpa, and Lord Caitanya consulted him about taking *sannyāsa*. Soon after Keśava Bhāratī's departure, Lord Caitanya clandestinely left home in the middle of the night, swam across the Gaṅgā, and proceeded toward Katwa, about thirty-five kilometers north of Navadvīpa, to be inducted as a sannyasi by Keśava Bhāratī.

Prior to taking *sannyāsa* Nimāi had to have His head shaved. Seeing beautiful Nimāi about to lose His long, wavy, glossy black hair, the local people tried to persuade Keśava Bhāratī not to give Him *sannyāsa*. Even the barber could not bring himself to shave the Lord's head. All present were overcome by the pain of imminent separation from the Lord. But Gaurāṅga was determined. Keśava Bhāratī then gave Him the *sannyāsa* name Śrī Kṛṣṇa Caitanya, which means "one who infuses Kṛṣṇa consciousness into others." Immediately thereafter Śrī Kṛṣṇa Caitanya left for Vṛndāvana, reciting from *Śrīmad-Bhāgavatam*, "I shall cross over the insurmountable ocean of nescience by being firmly fixed in the service of the lotus feet of Kṛṣṇa. This method was approved by previous *ācāryas* unshakably situated in devotion to the Supreme Personality of Godhead."

For three days and three nights Lord Caitanya walked along the bank of the Gaṅgā chanting Hare Kṛṣṇa. Absorbed in the prospect of going to Vṛndāvana, He knew not where He was, nor whether it was day or night. Nor was He aware that Nityānanda Prabhu, Mukunda, and another devotee were following Him. When He reached Kalna, across the Gaṅgā from

Śrī Kṛṣṇa Caitanya

Shantipur, the town where Advaita Ācārya lived, Lord Nityānanda told Mukunda, "Go ahead to Advaita Ācārya's house and tell Him to prepare for Śrī Kṛṣṇa Caitanya's visit." Then Nityānanda approached Lord Caitanya, who inquired, "Nitāi, how have You come here?" "I have been following You all this time," Nityānanda retorted.

"Please show Me where Vṛndāvana is," Lord Caitanya requested, to which Nityānanda replied, "This is Vṛndāvana." "Where is the Yamunā?" beckoned the Lord. "Right there. Just see the Yamunā," indicated Nityānanda, although actually it was the Gaṅgā.

As the two Lords walked toward the river They saw Advaita Ācārya coming across by boat. Lord Caitanya became suspicious. "How is Advaita Ācārya here? He lives in Shantipur. I think You have cheated Me. This is not the Yamunā and We are not in Vṛndāvana." Advaita Ācārya supplicated, "My dear Lord, wherever You are is Vṛndāvana, for You carry Vṛndāvana in Your heart."

Advaita Ācārya then brought Mahāprabhu to His house, where all the devotees from Navadvīpa had gathered. Knowing that they would no longer be seeing Him regularly, they wanted at least one more *darśana* of Gaurahari. Śacīmātā also had come. It was unbearable for her to see Nimāi with His head shaved. And now that He had taken a vow of renunciation she could no longer look after His comforts. Seeing her tears, the Lord agreed to stay there a few days so she could cook for Him. Thereupon a *saṅkīrtana* festival was arranged in the house of Advaita Ācārya. During the day the devotees would speak about Kṛṣṇa, and at night they would chant Hare Kṛṣṇa and take *prasāda* cooked by Śacīmātā.

After ten days Lord Caitanya declared, "I must leave. As a sannyasi I cannot stay surrounded by friends and relatives." "Then please stay in Purī," Śacīmātā requested. "People from Bengal regularly go to Purī, so if You reside there at least I will frequently get news about You."

Śrī Kṛṣṇa Caitanya agreed and left for Purī with Nityānanda, Jagadānanda, Mukunda, and Gadādhara. Along the way He chanted "Hari! Hari!" being overwhelmed with *kṛṣṇa-prema*. Sometimes He walked slowly, staggering as if intoxicated, sometimes He charged down the road like a lion, and sometimes He roared the holy names while dancing joyfully. Occasionally He would suddenly start crying. In transcendental madness He would hike up His dhoti and jump excitedly. Sometimes goose bumps covered His body from head to toe. Sometimes He laughed slowly and deeply.

Once when Lord Caitanya went to bathe in a river, He kept His *sannyāsa daṇḍa* (rod) with Nityānanda. Considering that Caitanya Mahāprabhu, the Supreme Personality of Godhead, did not need a *daṇḍa*—because He had taken *sannyāsa* as a matter of formality and was above the institution of *varṇāśrama-dharma*—Nityānanda broke the staff into three pieces and threw it in the river. When Lord Caitanya finished bathing He asked for His *daṇḍa.* Nityānanda replied, "You fell on it while dancing and it broke, so I threw it away." Knowing that Nityānanda was cheating Him, Gaurāṅga angrily avowed, "I will now leave all of you and go alone to Purī."

Nityānanda breaks the staff

Upon arriving in Purī, Mahāprabhu immediately went to the Jagannātha temple. During the whole trip His constant meditation had been on Lord Jagannātha (Kṛṣṇa). "When will I have *darśana* of Jagannātha? When will I see Kṛṣṇa, the Lord of My life?" Upon entering the temple, Mahāprabhu ran toward Jagannātha and fainted in ecstasy. The temple watchman became disturbed to see Him unconscious on the ground and moved forward as if to beat Him.

Fortunately Sārvabhauma Bhaṭṭācārya—the most famous *paṇḍita* in Purī and advisor to Mahārāja Pratāparudra, the king of Orissa—happened to be present and forbade anyone to mistreat this unknown sannyasi. Caitanya Mahāprabhu was so deeply stunned that Sārvabhauma feared He might be dead. Then the Bhaṭṭācārya had Him carried carefully to his home, where he tested the mendicant's breathing by holding a cotton swab under His nose. The cotton moved slightly, indicating that He was still alive.

A few hours later Nityānanda and the other devotees arrived in Purī and went straight to the temple, where they heard people talking of a beautiful golden-complexioned sannyasi who had come there, fainted, and been taken to the home of Sārvabhauma Bhaṭṭācārya. Soon after, Gopīnātha Ācārya, a pure devotee and the brother-in-law of Sārvabhauma Bhaṭṭācārya, also arrived there. Together they all proceeded to see the Lord. On reaching Sārvabhauma's home they found him worried. "This sannyasi has been unconscious for six hours," he stated.

The devotees knew exactly what to do. They loudly chanted Hare Kṛṣṇa, and after some time Lord Caitanya regained consciousness. Sārvabhauma was astonished to see all the symptoms of the highest *prema* in the body of the Lord and wanted to know about His background. Since Sārvabhauma originally hailed from the Navadvīpa area, he was pleased to hear from Gopīnātha Ācārya that Gaurāṅga was the son of Jagannātha Miśra. But Sārvabhauma objected when his brother-in-law declared Śrī Kṛṣṇa Caitanya to be the Supreme Lord. When after some scriptural discussion on this point Sārvabhauma remained unconvinced, Gopīnātha Ācārya averred, "The Supreme Personality of Godhead is in your home yet you cannot recognize Him."

Sārvabhauma was highly learned in Vedānta philosophy, and even though a householder, he used to teach sannyasis. Not understanding Lord Caitanya's supramundane position, and considering that because He was young and handsome it would be difficult for Him to maintain *sannyāsa*, Sārvabhauma proposed to teach Gaurāṅga impersonalistic Vedānta philosophy to fix Him in renunciation. But after expounding it for seven days Sārvabhauma inquired, "My dear sir, You listen to everything but never ask any question. Therefore I don't know whether or not You understand what I am saying."

"I understand Vedānta," Gaurāṅga replied, "albeit not your explanations. They make no sense." Sārvabhauma was shocked. Lord Caitanya continued, "A commentary should elucidate the meaning of the text, not cover it with another theory, as does yours. Vedānta clearly establishes the preeminence of

Sārvabhauma teaches Vedānta

the Supreme Personality of Godhead, yet you are obscuring its real import with false explanations."

Famed as the most authoritative Vedāntist of his day, Sārvabhauma presented innumerable arguments attempting to establish the absolute truth as *nirākāra* (without form, qualities, or names). Caitanya Mahāprabhu shattered his speculations one by one, until finally Sārvabhauma admitted defeat and bowed down to the Lord.

Being merciful to Sārvabhauma, the Lord showed him His six-armed manifestation: two arms of Lord Rāma holding a bow and arrows, two arms of Kṛṣṇa holding a flute, and His own two arms holding a sannyasi's staff and waterpot. Exulting in the compassion shown to him, the Bhaṭṭācārya abandoned his pursuit of dry logic and became a leading associate of Lord Caitanya's.

Six-armed manifestation

Chapter Five

South India Tour

Thereafter Gaurāṅga proposed to tour South India, on the pretext of searching for His elder brother Viśvarūpa, who had not been heard of since taking *sannyāsa* and leaving home. Yet Gaurāṅga's real reason for going to South India was to convert everyone there to the path of unalloyed devotion to the Supreme Lord Kṛṣṇa. Although all of Caitanya Mahāprabhu's devotees in Purī, headed by Nityānanda Prabhu, wanted to accompany the Lord, He nonetheless insisted on going alone. But the devotees successfully entreated Him to take at least one servant, Kālā Kṛṣṇadāsa. And at Sārvabhauma's request the Lord agreed to meet in course of His travels the great devotee Rāmānanda Rāya, governor of the southern extension of Pratāparudra's domain.

In one of the villages along Mahāprabhu's route lived a devotee named Vāsudeva. His body was rotting from leprosy, with worms

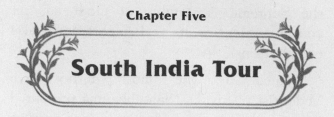

Vāsudeva meets the Lord

eating it, but being an exalted devotee he accepted his situation as due to past misdeeds. He understood that the best remedial measure for his plight was to devotedly chant Hare Kṛṣṇa while tolerating bodily pain. Vāsudeva was fully self-realized, understanding himself to be a spirit soul separate from his body. Whenever a worm dropped from his body he would put it back, thinking that otherwise the worm would perish.

Somehow Vāsudeva missed seeing Mahāprabhu, and in lamentation fell to the ground unconscious. To alleviate His devotee's distress the omniscient Lord immediately returned and embraced him, upon which Vāsudeva became cured and beautiful. Vāsudeva then prayed, "My dear Lord, now that I have this wonderful form, I beg not to become proud and forget that the purpose of life is to satisfy Kṛṣṇa." Lord Caitanya granted him these benedictions.

Traversing the paths of South India, Śrī Kṛṣṇa Caitanya would chant:

kṛṣṇa kṛṣṇa kṛṣṇa kṛṣṇa kṛṣṇa kṛṣṇa kṛṣṇa he!
kṛṣṇa kṛṣṇa kṛṣṇa kṛṣṇa kṛṣṇa kṛṣṇa kṛṣṇa he!
kṛṣṇa kṛṣṇa kṛṣṇa kṛṣṇa kṛṣṇa kṛṣṇa rakṣa mām
kṛṣṇa kṛṣṇa kṛṣṇa kṛṣṇa kṛṣṇa kṛṣṇa pāhi mām
rāma rāghava rāma rāghava rāma rāghava rākṣa mām
kṛṣṇa keśava kṛṣṇa keśava kṛṣṇa keśava pāhi mām

"O Lord Kṛṣṇa, protect Me and maintain Me. O Lord Rāma, descendant of King Raghu, protect Me. O Kṛṣṇa, O Keśava, killer of the Keśī demon, maintain Me."

Lord Caitanya's charming appearance enraptured all who beheld Him. One *brāhmaṇa* became so attracted that he wanted to immediately give up everything and follow Him. "My dear Lord," he prayed, "I am simply engrossed in materialistic family life. Please deliver me by letting me travel with You." But Lord Caitanya replied, "No, stay here. Chant Hare Kṛṣṇa, preach to others, and make them devotees. Wherever you go, whomever you meet, just instruct him about Kṛṣṇa. In this way, on My order become a guru and deliver this land. If you follow My instruction you will never be afflicted by the miseries of material life, and will again meet Me in this place; in other words, you will never be separated from Me."

Wherever Mahāprabhu went He would ask the people to chant Hare Kṛṣṇa. Suffused with Kṛṣṇa consciousness, those people would then go to another village and imbue others with Kṛṣṇa consciousness, who in turn would infuse still others with Kṛṣṇa consciousness. In this manner the chanting of Hare Kṛṣṇa spread all over South India.

On the bank of the river Godāvarī, Mahāprabhu met Rāmānanda Rāya and soon entered into profound theological discussion with him. The all-knowing independent Lord chose to ask questions while inwardly inspiring Rāmānanda Rāya to give perfect answers. To the first query, "What is the goal of life and the means to attain it?" Rāmānanda Rāya replied, "By observing duties within the *varṇāśrama* system every person can attain success." Mahāprabhu rebutted, "That is external. Please say something more."

Rāmānanda Rāya then described progressively superior processes. He suggested working without attachment to results, but

Gaurāṅga meets Rāmānanda Rāya on the bank of Godāvarī

Gaurāṅga disagreed. Next he advocated giving up one's duties in the *varṇāśrama* system, which Lord Caitanya also declined. Thereafter Rāmānanda proposed the path of cultivating knowledge, yet Mahāprabhu rejected that too. Then Rāmānanda Rāya said, "By pure devotion to Kṛṣṇa, free from the endeavor for sense gratification or empirical knowledge, one can attain success." Lord Caitanya accepted this as a suitable answer but requested, "Please tell Me still more."

Over the course of several nights Rāmānanda continued to describe progressive stages of Kṛṣṇa consciousness, up to the point of the intimate pastimes and emotions of Rādhā and Kṛṣṇa. Then Lord Caitanya revealed His original form as Rādhā-Kṛṣṇa to Rāmānanda Rāya. Mahāprabhu and Rāmānanda relished the bliss of discussing Kṛṣṇa in each other's company. "Please stay here longer so we can converse more," Rāmānanda pleaded. Lord Caitanya replied, "I want that together we relish these topics not only for a few days but throughout the rest of our lives. Yet first I have some preaching duties in South India. After some time I shall return to Purī. Meanwhile please get free from your responsibilities and proceed to Purī, where we shall live together."

Rādhā-Kṛṣṇa form

Mahāprabhu then pilgrimaged to many holy places: Ahobilam, Tirupati, Shri Shailam, Kanchipuram, Srirangam, Madurai, Kumbhakonam, Tanjore, Rameswaram, Kanyakumari, and more. He visited not only Viṣṇu temples but also those of demigods, seeing them not as independent gods but as prominent devotees of the Supreme Lord Kṛṣṇa and, on that basis, worthy of worship. He bathed in holy rivers and preached Kṛṣṇa consciousness village to village. Each night He would stay in a temple and present Vaiṣṇava philosophy to the local *paṇḍitas*. And He would induce the general populace to chant Hare Kṛṣṇa.

By the time Lord Caitanya reached Srirangam, Cāturmāsya had begun, and He accepted the invitation of the local *brāhmaṇa* Vyeṅkaṭa Bhaṭṭa to stay at his house throughout its duration.* The devotees of Śrī Raṅganātha considered themselves blessed to have Gaurāṅga in their midst, and were especially pleased to see Him dance and chant in ecstasy before the deity in the temple. Every day different *brāhmaṇas* would invite Him for lunch.

Once Mahāprabhu joked with Vyeṅkaṭa Bhaṭṭa, "Your object of worship, Lakṣmī, always remains on the chest of Nārāyaṇa, and she is certainly the most chaste woman in the

* Cāturmāsya—four-month period of the monsoon, when mud and rain make traveling difficult and mendicants usually remain in a holy place to observe vows of austerity. Srirangam is the home of the Viṣṇu deity Śrī Raṅganātha and a major Vaiṣṇava center.

creation. But My Lord is Śrī Kṛṣṇa, a cowherd boy. Chaste wife that she is, why does Lakṣmī want to associate with My Lord? To attain that end, she abandoned the transcendental happiness of Vaikuṇṭha and accepted prolonged vows and unlimited austerities."

Vyeṅkaṭa Bhaṭṭa replied, "Lord Kṛṣṇa and Lord Nārāyaṇa are one and the same, yet the pastimes of Kṛṣṇa are more delightful due to their sportive nature. Since Kṛṣṇa and Nārāyaṇa are the same personality, Lakṣmī's desiring Kṛṣṇa did not break her vow of chastity. Rather, it was in great fun that the goddess of fortune wanted to unite with Lord Kṛṣṇa and relish the *rāsa* dance.* If she wanted to enjoy herself with Kṛṣṇa what fault is there? Why are You joking so about this?"

Mahāprabhu responded, "There is no defect in Lakṣmī, but still she could not participate in the *rāsa* dance. Can you tell me why, despite being the goddess of fortune, she could not get that opportunity?" To this Vyeṅkaṭa Bhaṭṭa replied, "I cannot enter into the mystery of this incident. I am an

---

* *Rāsa* dance, *rāsa-līlā*—famous dance of Kṛṣṇa with the *gopīs* of Vṛndāvana, considered to be the pinnacle of spiritual bliss in transcendental loving exchanges.

ordinary living being. How can I understand the activities of the Supreme Lord? They are deeper than millions of oceans."

Then Lord Caitanya explained that Lakṣmī could not join *rāsa-līlā* due to her attitude of reverential worship of the Supreme Lord. In Vaikuṇṭha awe and reverence for the Lord prevails, whereas Vṛndāvana is a place of simple and natural love for Kṛṣṇa. Vṛndāvana is characterized by fruits, flowers, cows, and the river Yamunā. The atmosphere there is intimate rather than respectful. But Lakṣmī could not give up her Vaikuṇṭha mood, nor was she prepared to follow the standard process for entering Kṛṣṇa's *rāsa-līlā:* to relinquish her Vaikuṇṭha form, accept that of a cowherd girl, and follow in the footsteps of the residents of Vṛndāvana. Thus, in a humorous manner Lord Caitanya clarified how worship of Kṛṣṇa is higher than worship of Lakṣmī-Nārāyaṇa, and the mood of intimacy superior to awe and reverence. But then He said, "Do not feel bad. We are simply joking. I am not admonishing you."

In the Srirangam temple compound Mahāprabhu once saw a *brāhmaṇa* sitting and crying with *Bhagavad-gītā* in his hands.

Some people were laughing at him. Seeing this Lord Caitanya asked, "My dear sir, what are you doing and why are you weeping?" The *brāhmaṇa* replied, "My guru told me to daily recite *Bhagavad-gītā*, yet actually I am uneducated. Even though I was born a *brāhmaṇa*, I don't know how to read properly. Yet I try to read as well as I can."

Mahāprabhu asked, "So why are you crying?"

"Actually," replied the *brāhmaṇa*, "I only see Lord Kṛṣṇa sitting on a chariot, as Arjuna's driver. Taking the reins in His hands He appears very beautiful and blackish. While beholding Lord Kṛṣṇa instructing Arjuna, my heart becomes overwhelmed and I cannot restrain my tears." Gaurāṅga embraced the *brāhmaṇa*, assuring him, "Even though you cannot read properly, you are a true student of *Bhagavad-gītā*, for you have understood its message."

While wandering near Madurai, Mahāprabhu came to the home of a surrendered devotee of Lord Rāma who was always sad, thinking how Rāvaṇa had kidnapped Mother Sītā, as described in the epic *Rāmāyaṇa*. Lord Caitanya consoled him, "Actually I think it was not possible for Rāvaṇa to take away Sītā." Some days later, while visiting Rāmeśvaram, Gaurāṅga found an ancient manuscript of the *Kūrma Purāṇa*, which describes that Rāvaṇa had taken not the actual Sītā but an illusory representation, and that while separated from Rāma her original form was protected by the demigod Agni. Lord Caitanya brought the relevant page of the *Kūrma Purāṇa* to the grieving devotee, who, now relieved of distress, declared, "Although You appear to be a sannyasi, actually You are my dearmost Lord Rāma."

Gradually Mahāprabhu reached the west coast of South India, where He visited holy places such as Thiruvanantapuram, Udupi, and Shringeri. During this period a gang of Bhaṭṭathāris, a nomadic community possessed of tantric black arts, brought Kālā Kṛṣṇadāsa into their fold by alluring his mind with women. When Mahāprabhu went to rescue His servant the Bhaṭṭathāris attacked Him, but the weapons they threw came back and struck their own bodies. Mahāprabhu then grabbed Kālā Kṛṣṇadāsa by the hair and forcefully dragged him back into His company. This incident indicates that if one is not sufficiently serious about Kṛṣṇa consciousness, then even in the direct association of the Supreme Personality of Godhead he can succumb to illusion.

Chapter Six

Return to Purī, and Pastimes at Ratha-yātrā

When after two years Śrī Caitanya Mahāprabhu returned to Purī, His devotees felt as if they had regained their life. Lord Caitanya first met Nityānanda, Jagadānanda, Mukunda, and Sārvabhauma Bhaṭṭācārya. "I visited many holy places and spoke with many saintly people," He informed Sārvabhauma, "but I could not find anyone of Rāmānanda Rāya's caliber. By discussing *kṛṣṇa-kathā* with him I achieved much enlightenment and ecstasy." At the house of Kāśī Miśra, the king's guru, Sārvabhauma arranged a room for Lord Caitanya which, although conveniently close to the Jagannātha temple, was nonetheless peaceful and secluded. Kāśī Miśra was delighted to have the Lord staying at his home.

In expectation of Mahāprabhu's return, many devotees had come to Purī from different places, and on hearing of His arrival they rushed to see Him. One of them,

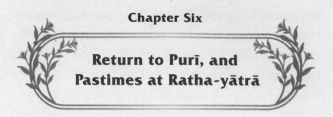

Govinda, requested, "My dear Lord, please let me spend my life in Your personal service." At first Gaurāṅga hesitated because Govinda was His godbrother, from whom acceptance of service is proscribed by rules of etiquette. But after Govinda explained that he had been instructed by Īśvara Purī to serve Him, the Lord accepted, for the order of the spiritual master supersedes other considerations. In countless ways Govinda faithfully tended the Lord until His departure from the world.

Although Mahāprabhu had rescued Kālā Kṛṣṇadāsa, He no longer wanted him in His company. He told His associates, "This man was unfaithful and abandoned Me, so I don't want to see him ever again." Hearing this, Kālā Kṛṣṇadāsa wept. But the devotees headed by Lord Nityānanda found a way to keep Kālā Kṛṣṇadāsa engaged in devotional service. With Mahāprabhu's permission they sent Kālā Kṛṣṇadāsa to Bengal to inform the devotees there that the Lord had returned and they could visit Him in Purī.

Just after Viśvambhara took *sannyāsa*, Puruṣottama Ācārya from Navadvīpa also left home, went to Varanasi, and there took *sannyāsa*. After some time he came to Purī.

Now known as Svarūpa, he submitted himself to Caitanya Mahāprabhu. Gaurāṅga joyfully greeted him and added the name Dāmodara to his *sannyāsa* name. Svarūpa Dāmodara stayed with the Lord constantly and became His most confidential associate. He was a vastly learned scholar and the foremost authority among Mahāprabhu's followers. Even when other devotees sometimes had philosophical misunderstandings, Svarūpa Dāmodara was never bewildered and would correct their mistakes. He was so intimate with the Lord that he intuitively understood His emotions, and would sweetly sing confidential devotional songs to enhance Gaurāṅga's devotional moods.

Upon hearing of the wonderful activities and intense devotion of Lord Caitanya, the king of Orissa, Pratāparudra Mahārāja, became eager to meet Him. But considering it improper for a sannyasi to mix with a monarch, Caitanya Mahāprabhu refused, declaring, "Alas, for a person who seriously desires to cross the material ocean and engage in the transcendental loving service of the Lord without material motives, to see a materialist engaged in sense gratification, or a woman similarly interested, is more despicable than willingly drinking poison."

Deeply disappointed, the king had Sārvabhauma Bhaṭṭācārya and Rāmānanda Rāya repeatedly petition Gaurāṅga to grant him an audience. Yet as much as the king was ardent to meet Him, the Lord was adamant not to. He even threatened His devotees that if they continued to pressure Him, He would simply leave Purī and not return. When Sārvabhauma relayed this to Pratāparudra Mahārāja, the disheartened king lamented, "When Lord Caitanya was in South India He bestowed mercy even to trees, for by embracing seven palm stalks He sent them to Vaikuṇṭha. Has Mahāprabhu vowed to deliver all sinners except the wretched soul called Pratāparudra? If Gaurahari is not compassionate to me, I shall give up my kingdom, become a mendicant, and beg from door to door." But Gaurahari remained intransigent, and the king remained disappointed yet still hopeful of some day achieving His mercy.

Ratha-yātrā is a popular festival in which Lord Jagannātha leaves His temple and is pulled on a large chariot to another temple, called Guṇḍicā. Traditionally many pilgrims journey from Bengal to Purī to attend

Ratha-yātrā. Similarly, after Gaurāṅga took up residence in Purī, most of His married devotees from Bengal made an annual pilgrimage to visit Him at Ratha-yātrā and remain throughout the four months of the monsoon.

The first year, they went in a group of about two hundred. Upon arriving they were delighted to see Sārvabhauma Bhaṭṭācārya, previously famed as a leading impersonalist, dancing and chanting in their midst. Mahārāja Pratāparudra asked to have the devotees pointed out to him, so Gopīnātha Ācārya took him to the roof of the palace, from where they could see the devotees singing the holy names in the streets of Purī. Gopīnātha Ācārya identified all the chief devotees to the king, who was astonished upon seeing their bodily luster and the extraordinary fervor with which they chanted Hare Kṛṣṇa. He had heard many *kīrtanas*, but their chanting made the hairs of his body stand on end and much increased his eagerness to meet Gaurāṅga.

Shortly thereafter Haridāsa Ṭhākura arrived from Bengal. Even though a reputed devotee, because of his birth in a Muslim family he was not allowed to enter the Jagannātha temple. So Mahāprabhu arranged

Haridāsa Ṭhākura

a room for him wherefrom he could see the *cakra* of the temple and offer obeisances to it.* Mahāprabhu also arranged for him to daily receive *mahā-prasāda* of Lord Jagannātha. And although Haridāsa Ṭhākura was not allowed to see Jagannātha in the temple, each day Jagannātha in His form as Lord Caitanya would personally go to meet him, thus demonstrating that even if a fully surrendered devotee is restricted from seeing the Lord, the Lord will come to see him.

Although the Lord regularly visited Haridāsa, He still refused to meet Mahārāja Pratāparudra. Unable to endure this, the king repeatedly requested Rāmānanda Rāya to arrange an audience. By repeatedly extolling the saintly qualities of Pratāparudra, Rāmānanda Rāya was eventually able to convince Caitanya Mahāprabhu that this ruler was not simply materialistic, but actually a serious devotee. Although the Lord's stance

---

* *Cakra*—wheel. Specially designed *cakras* placed atop Viṣṇu temples are considered nondifferent from His disc weapon and thus as venerable as He.

gradually softened, He remained cautious about meeting a monarch. Nonetheless, at Nityānanda's request He sent Mahārāja Pratāparudra mercy in the form of a cloth He had worn. Mahārāja Pratāparudra then undertook worship of Gaurāṅga's garment as if it were the Lord Himself. Thereafter Mahāprabhu said, "According to scripture the son represents the father, so the prince's meeting Me will be just as good as the king's seeing Me." The devotees then brought the young prince to Lord Caitanya. The boy was beautiful, blackish in complexion, and had large lotus eyes. He wore yellow cloth and his body was decorated with jeweled ornaments. Upon seeing him Gaurāṅga was reminded of Kṛṣṇa, and with deep affection embraced the youth. Although this partially satisfied Mahārāja Pratāparudra, he still yearned for Mahāprabhu's direct audience.

Each year on the day before Ratha-yātrā, Lord Caitanya and His associates would clean the Guṇḍicā temple, to prepare for Lord Jagannātha's visit. Taking hundreds of brooms and water pots, they thoroughly swept the temple and its surrounding area twice, threw water everywhere, and washed the temple inside and out. By this pastime Lord Caitanya demonstrated that all dirt within the heart of a devotee must be removed before Kṛṣṇa will consent to manifest Himself therein.

Cleaning the Guṇḍicā temple

On Ratha-yātrā day Lord Jagannātha was carried from the temple and seated on His cart. Mahāprabhu was calling out *Maṇimā! Maṇimā!* but could not be heard due to the tumultuous sound of various musical instruments.* Even though master of the kingdom, Pratāparudra Mahārāja considered himself a menial servant of Lord Jagannātha. Therefore just before the parade began he swept the road with a golden broom. This humble act endeared him to Lord Caitanya.

Seven *saṅkīrtana* parties accompanied the procession. When Gaurāṅga beheld Lord Jagannātha's smiling face He began jumping and dancing in all seven groups simultaneously. Most devotees thought

* *Maṇimā*—Oriya term for addressing an honored personality.

Saṅkīrtana parties jumping and dancing

Mahāprabhu was present in their group only, but His most confidential associates could understand that He had expanded Himself into seven forms. Because Mahārāja Pratāparudra's manifest humility had pleased Lord Caitanya, he received special mercy in being able to perceive the Lord's concurrent dancing in all the *kīrtana* groups. Gaurāṅga appeared like a golden mountain leaping in the air, causing the entire earth to tilt.

Lord Caitanya next offered various scriptural prayers to Jagannātha and also recited what seemed like a mundane love poem, the meaning of which only Svarūpa Dāmodara could understand. But later Śrīla Rūpa

Gosvāmī explained its purport: Mahāprabhu was cherishing the mood of Śrīmatī Rādhārāṇī when She and the residents of Vṛndāvana met Kṛṣṇa at Kurukṣetra many years after He had left Vṛndāvana. Kṛṣṇa now wore the royal dress of the king of Dvārakā and was surrounded by soldiers, elephants, and other signs of opulence. Seeing Him after so many years, Rādhārāṇī lamented that although She had again achieved His association, She could not relate intimately with Him in such a regal and crowded atmosphere. She yearned to take Him back to the simple rural ambiance of Vṛndāvana. Mahāprabhu was undergoing Rādhārāṇī's trauma of separation from Kṛṣṇa, and experiencing Ratha-yātrā as an emotional process of bringing Kṛṣṇa—now in the form of Lord Jagannātha—from Dvārakā, represented by the Jagannātha temple, back to Vṛndāvana, represented by the Guṇḍicā temple.

Lord Caitanya addressed Jagannātha, "You are the same Kṛṣṇa and I am the same Rādhārāṇī. We are meeting again in the same way that We met in the beginning of Our lives. Although We are the same persons, My mind is still attracted to Vṛndāvana. I therefore request You to come to Vṛndāvana and enjoy pastimes with Me. If You do so, My ambition will be fulfilled."

When the Lord was dancing before Jagannātha's cart, He sometimes moved ahead quickly. Jagannātha would then quickly follow behind Him. And when Mahāprabhu moved slowly, Jagannātha moved slowly. In the mood of Rādhārāṇī, Lord Caitanya was controlling Kṛṣṇa and leading Him to Vṛndāvana.

Halfway along the route Lord Jagannātha stopped His cart to rest for a while. Tired from dancing, Mahāprabhu entered a garden to relax under a tree. As previously advised by Sārvabhauma Bhaṭṭācārya, Mahārāja Pratāparudra entered the garden dressed as a humble Vaiṣṇava in simple cloth and without ornaments. Taking permission from the devotees present, he massaged Lord Caitanya's legs and feet and chanted the exquisite "Song of the Gopīs" from *Śrīmad-Bhāgavatam.* Upon hearing the ninth verse, Gaurāṅga arose in ecstasy, hugged the king, and declared, "You have given Me priceless gems, but I have nothing to give you in return. Therefore I am simply embracing you." Then He repeatedly recited this stanza in an overflow of transcendental love:

Mahārāja Pratāparudra massages Lord Caitanya's legs and feet

My Lord, the nectar of Your words and the descriptions of Your activities are the life and soul of those who are always aggrieved in this material world. Transmitted by exalted personalities, these narrations eradicate all sinful reactions, and whoever hears them attains all good fortune. Such recitations are broadcast all over the world and are filled with spiritual power. Those who spread the message of Godhead are certainly the most munificent welfare workers.

"You are the most munificent! You are the most munificent!" Lord Caitanya exclaimed. Again He embraced the king and bestowed His full mercy upon him. Although He knew everything, He pretended not to know that He was talking with the disguised monarch.

After Jagannātha had resumed His journey and His chariot been moving for some time, it suddenly stopped. Despite hundreds of men tugging the ropes with all their might, it did not budge. Big strong men were brought to pull—but in vain. Even elephants, despite being prodded until they screamed, could not budge it. Nobody knew what to do. Actually, Lord Jagannātha allows Himself to be transported just to give His devotees a chance to serve Him, yet He moves by His own will and when He wants to stop, He stops. Gaurāṅga then went behind the cart and pushed with His head. The chariot slowly rumbled forward again and Jagannātha resumed His stroll. The *kīrtana* became even more tumultuous and

Gaurāṅga pushes the cart with His head

continued up to the Guṇḍicā temple, where Jagannātha dismounted.

Five days after the Ratha-yātrā festival is Herā-pañcamī, when the goddess of fortune, angry at her husband's absence, comes to Guṇḍicā to try to bring Him back home. On that day Śrīvāsa Paṇḍita extolled the glories of Vaikuṇṭha and the goddess of fortune, but Svarūpa Dāmodara retorted, "My dear Śrīvāsa, the combined opulences of Dvārakā and Vaikuṇṭha are paltry compared to those of Vṛndāvana." To support this assertion Svarūpa Dāmodara quoted a verse from *Brahma-saṁhitā* (5.56): "The *gopīs* of Vṛndāvana are super goddesses of fortune. The enjoyer in Vṛndāvana is the Supreme Personality of Godhead, Kṛṣṇa. The trees fulfil all desires and the land is made of transcendental thought-gems. The water is nectar, the talking is singing, the walking is dancing, and the constant companion of Kṛṣṇa is His flute. Therefore Vṛndāvana is the only relishable abode."

The devotees from Bengal remained in Purī throughout the four months of the monsoon. Immersed in the happiness of Lord Caitanya's sweet company, they celebrated various festivals for the pleasure of Lord Jagannātha.

Then Gaurāṅga requested them to return to Bengal. He specifically asked Nityānanda and Advaita to bestow *kṛṣṇa-prema* upon all of them, without consideration of caste or creed. But the devotees had no desire to relinquish Mahāprabhu's association. Although every day they would prepare to go, they could not bring themselves to depart. Finally Lord Caitanya insisted that they return to their duties. He assured them, "Even while remaining in Purī, I shall simultaneously be present with you in Bengal, particularly when Śrīvāsa Paṇḍita holds *kīrtana* in his home and whenever Nityānanda performs His blissful dancing. I also go daily to Navadvīpa to see the lotus feet of my mother. She is able to feel My presence, although she does not believe it to be actual."

As the devotees from the village of Kulina-gram, Bengal, were about to depart, the Lord asked them to bring strong silk ropes every year for pulling the Ratha-yātrā carts. Satyarāja Khan then beseeched Gaurāṅga, "My dear Lord, being a materialistic householder I do not know how to advance in spiritual life. Kindly instruct me." Lord Caitanya directed him to unceasingly chant the holy name of Kṛṣṇa and to serve the Lord and His devotees. Satyarāja then inquired,

"How can I recognize a devotee? What are his characteristics?" Mahāprabhu explained that the primary attribute of a Vaiṣṇava is his renouncing the association of nondevotees. When Satyarāja asked for more details, Lord Caitanya elucidated that anyone who even once chants the holy name of Lord Kṛṣṇa is a Vaiṣṇava.

When Satyarāja Khan visited Purī the next year he inquired further about the characteristics of Vaiṣṇavas, and this time Mahāprabhu replied that anyone who constantly chants the name of Kṛṣṇa is a Vaiṣṇava. And when a year later Satyarāja Khan again asked the very same question, Gaurāṅga replied, "A Vaiṣṇava is one whose mere presence inspires others to chant the names of Kṛṣṇa." In this way Lord Caitanya gradually described the three levels of Vaiṣṇavas: neophyte, intermediate, and topmost.

The great devotee Vāsudeva Datta supplicated Mahāprabhu, "My Lord, I cannot bear to see the conditioned souls suffer. Please transfer the karma of their sinful lives upon my head. Let me suffer perpetually in a hellish condition for their sinful reactions, but kindly deliver them from their diseased material life." Exceedingly satisfied with Vāsudeva Datta,

Lord Caitanya embraced him. "Whatever a pure devotee wants from his master," He declared, "Lord Kṛṣṇa surely grants. Kṛṣṇa's only duty is to fulfil the desire of His devotees. So if you desire the liberation of all living entities within the universe, it can be effected without your undergoing the tribulations of karmic punishment. Kṛṣṇa possesses all potencies. Why would He let you endure the sinful reactions of other living entities?"

Among altruists Vāsudeva Datta stands supreme, far above all mundane philanthropists, philosophers, and worldly heroes, because his desire to benefit others was not limited to a certain group or species but extended to every living being in the creation. Furthermore, the welfare he desired for them was the highest—to be delivered from material existence and go back home, back to Godhead.

Chapter Seven

Travels in North India

Although Gaurāṅga repeatedly expressed a desire to go to Vṛndāvana, on one pretext or another His followers would detain Him. Yet eventually He received their permission and thus set out for Vṛndāvana via Bengal. When He arrived in the Navadvīpa area He did not go to His former home, but stayed on the other side of the Gaṅgā.

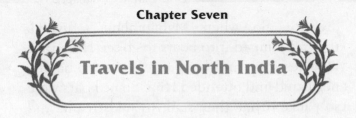

The inhabitants of Navadvīpa had become thunderstruck when their Nimāi suddenly left to take *sannyāsa*. Upon hearing that Mahārāja Pratāparudra, the famous independent Hindu king of Orissa, and the vastly learned Sārvabhauma Bhaṭṭācārya had become Gaurāṅga's followers, and that He had converted innumerable people to Vaiṣṇavism all over South India, the people of Navadvīpa felt immense pride, but also remorse for not previously recognizing His greatness. Even those who had opposed the Lord's *saṅkīrtana* movement were now lamenting His departure and their inability to have discerned His divinity. So when Mahāprabhu returned, they all jumped into boats to go see Him, take His blessings, and beg forgiveness for having neglected and offended Him. Some boats were so packed that they sank in midstream, and some persons were so eager to see the Lord that, unable to wait for a boat, they simply swam across the river. Wherever Māhaprabhu went, huge crowds would fall at His lotus feet. At each spot where those feet touched the ground, numerous holes were created by so many people scooping up the sanctified dust.

This excited multitude followed Gaurāṅga as He proceeded north toward Ramakeli, near the then capital of Bengal. The Muslim king was astonished to hear how a sannyasi accompanied by thousands of Hindus was approaching his capital. "He must be a prophet," he thought, "for how could a mere mendicant attract so many people?" He ordered his magistrate not to disturb this saint. He then asked another trusted assistant, Keśava Chatri, about Śrī Caitanya Mahāprabhu. Afraid that the king was considering retributive action, Keśava Chatri tried to avoid the subject by stating that the Lord was merely a sadhu touring different places of pilgrimage and only a few people were going to see Him. But not satisfied with this answer the monarch privately asked his finance minister, Dabir Khas, his opinion of the sannyasi. "Why are you questioning me?" the minister replied. "Better you examine your own mind. As a king, you represent the Supreme Lord. Therefore you can understand better than I." "Śrī Caitanya Mahāprabhu is the Supreme Personality of Godhead," the king replied. "I am sure of it."

After this exchange Dabir Khas returned to his residence and consulted with his elder brother Sakar Mallik, who was the prime minister. Although born in a high-class *brāhmaṇa* family, the brothers had been obliged to work in the Muslim government and had eventually adopted Muslim names and customs. Considering themselves contaminated, they yearned for the association of Lord Caitanya.

In the dead of night the two brothers secretly went to see the Lord. Clasping clumps of straw in their mouths as a sign of humility, they fell flat at His feet and offered prayers describing their degraded condition and begging for His causeless mercy. "Dear Lord, let us inform you that no one is more sinful than us, nor is there any offender like us. Even if we wanted to mention our sinful activities, we would immediately become ashamed. And what to speak of giving them up! You have incarnated to deliver the fallen souls. You should consider that in this world there is none so fallen as us." The Lord replied, "My dear Dabir Khas and Sakar Mallik, you two brothers are My eternal servants. From this day you will be known as Rūpa and Sanātana. Please abandon your humility, for it is breaking My heart. I came to Bengal just to see you. I had no other reason to come. Now you can go home. Do not fear anything, for Kṛṣṇa will soon deliver you."

Before leaving, Rūpa and Sanātana respectfully suggested that it would be inappropriate for the Lord to journey to Vṛndāvana with a crowd of followers. Accordingly Mahāprabhu revised His program and returned to Purī.

Rūpa and Sanātana decided to renounce their government posts to engage fully in the service of Lord Caitanya. Rūpa left first. He settled his family affairs and divided his wealth by giving fifty percent to *brāhmaṇas* and Vaiṣṇavas and twenty-five percent to relatives. He kept the remaining twenty-five percent for personal emergencies. Foreseeing Sanātana's needs, he also deposited ten thousand gold coins with a local merchant and then set out to meet Śrī Caitanya Mahāprabhu.

Sanātana Gosvāmī could not leave so easily. The king depended on him to run the administration and refused to let him go. When Sanātana insisted on quitting, the king imprisoned him. Sanātana managed to escape by bribing the jail keeper with seven thousand of Rūpa's gold coins. Covertly crossing mountain ranges, he hastened to meet Lord Caitanya.

Meanwhile Gaurāṅga had returned to Purī. Yet before long He again became anxious to visit Vṛndāvana, this time without a retinue. At His associates' request, He agreed to accept one assistant, the gentle and learned *brāhmaṇa* Balabhadra Bhaṭṭācārya. Early one morning, unseen by others, they departed. Avoiding public roads, they traversed forest trails through the vast jungle of Jharkhand, which was full of tigers, elephants, and other wild animals. But without any cares or worries

Lord Caitanya happily chanted the names of Kṛṣṇa. From time to time they would come across forest hamlets, where Balabhadra would arrange meals with *brāhmaṇas*. Otherwise he would feed the Lord whatever fruits, roots, or leaves were available. Whenever they met aborigines, the Lord would happily induce them to chant Hare Kṛṣṇa.

One day while in a rapturous trance, Gaurāṅga unknowingly trod on a sleeping tiger, who stirred and awakened. "Now we are finished!" Balabhadra thought. But Gaurāṅga ordered the tiger, "Get up! Why are you sleeping? Chant Hare Kṛṣṇa!" The tiger rose and started chanting Hare Kṛṣṇa, suffused with transcendental joy. Another time, while Lord Caitanya was bathing in a river a herd of mad elephants arrived. The Lord splashed them with water and asked them to chant Hare Kṛṣṇa. When the water touched their bodies the elephants began chanting "Kṛṣṇa! Kṛṣṇa!" Some of them danced, some fell to the ground, and others screamed in ecstasy.

Often Mahāprabhu's sweet singing would attract deer to come and follow Him. One day some tigers joined the party, and when Lord Caitanya ordered them to chant Hare Kṛṣṇa, the tigers and deer danced and chanted

Mahāprabhu makes the animals dance in saṅkīrtana

"Kṛṣṇa!" embracing and kissing one another while the astounded Balabhadra looked on. All the animals, birds, and even trees and creepers that He met along the jungle path were awakened to jubilant love of Kṛṣṇa.

Eventually Gaurāṅga arrived in Varanasi, where He met Tapana Miśra, the *brāhmaṇa* from East Bengal whom He had instructed about chanting the holy names. On the Lord's order Tapana Miśra had moved to Varanasi, but he was morose because that city was full of Māyāvādīs and there were few devotees to associate with. Mahāprabhu accepted Tapana Miśra's invitation to have lunch at his place for ten days.

Gaurahari then proceeded toward Mathurā. Upon seeing the city He immediately fell to the ground and offered obeisances. After entering Mathurā He bathed in the Yamunā, visited the birthplace of Kṛṣṇa, and saw the ancient deity Keśavaji. Although always merged in the bliss of remembering Kṛṣṇa's transcendentally joyful pastimes in Vṛndāvana, Lord Caitanya's ecstasy increased a thousand times when He reached Mathurā and a hundred thousand times when He actually entered Vṛndāvana. His mind saturated in loving separation from Kṛṣṇa, Mahāprabhu walked through the twelve forests of Vṛndāvana. As He proceeded, all the flora and fauna recognized that the Lord of their lives, Kṛṣṇa, had returned in the form of a golden sannyasi, and they happily reciprocated with Him. Mooing loudly, herds of grazing cows surrounded Him and licked His body in great affection. Does and bucks also came to lick and accompany Him. Parrots, cuckoos, and bumblebees sang loudly and peacocks danced before Him. Even the trees and creepers became jubilant and, shedding tears of love in the form of honey, offered their fruits and flowers at the Lord's lotus feet.

While in Mathurā, Mahāprabhu met a disciple of Mādhavendra Purī from the Sanodiya caste of *brāhmaṇas*. This devotee accompanied the Lord on His Vṛndāvana pilgrimage and gave Him lodging at his home, wherefrom Gaurāṅga daily went to Vṛndāvana.

One day as He sat by the Yamunā, the Lord suddenly jumped in and remained underwater for some time until Balabhadra pulled Him out. Fearing that similar mishaps might occur while Gaurāṅga wandered alone in Vṛndāvana, Balabhadra thus proposed to take Him to Prayāga. Not wanting to put His servant in anxiety, Mahāprabhu agreed to go.

Lord Caitanya, Balabhadra, the Sanodiya *brāhmaṇa*, and a Rajput devotee whom the Lord had met in Vṛndāvana, named Kṛṣṇadāsa, set off along the Yamunā's bank toward Prayāga. When a cowherd boy blew on his flute, Gaurāṅga took it to be Kṛṣṇa's flute and fainted. Just then ten Muslim Pathan cavalry soldiers rode up. Seeing the Lord unconscious with four men around Him, the soldiers dismounted and arrested them. "You must have poisoned this sannyasi to take His money," they reasoned. "Now we have caught you." Balabhadra and his assistant were trembling in fright, but Kṛṣṇadāsa, being from the princely caste and fearless, challenged the soldiers: "My home is nearby, and I have about two hundred Turkish soldiers and a hundred cannons. If I call loudly they will come immediately to kill you and plunder your horses and saddles." Hearing this, the Pathan soldiers became apprehensive.

Just then Lord Caitanya came to external consciousness and began chanting "Hari! Hari!" The Pathan soldiers submitted, "My dear Sir, these rogues have poisoned You to steal Your money." "I am a sannyasi," Mahāprabhu replied. "I don't have any money. And these are not rogues, they are My associates."

Gaurāṅga faints upon hearing a cowherd boy's flute

Accompanying the soldiers was a grave and saintly person, who tried to convince Gaurāṅga about the impersonal nature of God by citing the Koran, but the Lord refuted all his arguments. Then

Mahāprabhu gave evidence that although at first the Koran had established impersonalism, it later disproved it and established that the Personality of Godhead is the ultimate truth. The saintly Muslim and all the soldiers then surrendered to the Lord. Thereafter they became famous as the Pathan Vaiṣṇavas and preached Kṛṣṇa consciousness widely.

Although the city of Prayāga is situated at the confluence of the mighty rivers Gaṅgā and Yamunā, it never flooded until Mahāprabhu came and drowned it with *kṛṣṇa-prema.* It was now the month of Māgha (December–January), when saintly persons from all over North India gather at Triveṇī, where the Gaṅgā and Yamunā converge, to bathe at particular auspicious times. Thus thousands of people joined the Lord's *saṅkīrtana* movement during His stay in Prayāga.

Mahāprabhu would daily visit Bindu Mādhava, a noted temple of Lord Viṣṇu near the Triveṇī. When Rūpa Gosvāmī and his younger brother Anupama arrived at Prayāga, they saw Gaurāṅga on His way to the Bindu Mādhava temple. They immediately put clumps of straw between their teeth and fell flat on the ground, offering obeisances. The

Lord greeted and embraced them. With joined palms Rūpa Gosvāmī recited a verse that was to become a famous prayer:

namo mahā-vadānyāya kṛṣṇa-prema pradāya te
kṛṣṇāya kṛṣṇa-caitanya nāmne gaura-tviṣe namaḥ

> O most munificent avatar! You are Kṛṣṇa Himself appearing as Śrī Caitanya Mahāprabhu. You have assumed the golden color of Śrīmatī Rādhārāṇī and are widely distributing pure love of Kṛṣṇa. We offer our respectful obeisances unto You.

The purport of this prayer is most significant. Certainly many other avatars had mercifully descended to this mundane plane, but none were as magnanimous as Caitanya Mahāprabhu. He distributed very widely and without restriction the highest, most confidential, and otherwise exceedingly rarely achieved aspect of devotional service—conjugal love of Rādhā and Kṛṣṇa—to the

Most munificent incarnation

most fallen souls by the easiest and most joyful method of chanting the holy names. Gaurāṅga is even more merciful than in His previous appearance as Lord Kṛṣṇa, who simply instructed that everyone should become His devotee, for Mahāprabhu personally taught the process for attaining such pure Kṛṣṇa consciousness.

Vallabha Bhaṭṭa, the distinguished devotee and originator of the Puṣṭi-mārga sect of Vaiṣṇavism, lived on the opposite side of the Yamunā from Prayāga. Having heard that Lord Caitanya was in town he went to invite Him for lunch. Then Gaurāṅga introduced Vallabha to Rūpa and Anupama. Aware of his aristocratic lineage, the Lord advised Vallabha not to touch Rūpa and Anupama, because they were of low caste. Vallabha Bhaṭṭa understood that the Lord was subtly instructing him. "Since these two are constantly chanting the holy name of Kṛṣṇa," he responded, "how can they be untouchable? On the contrary, they are most exalted." Vallabha Bhaṭṭa then quoted a verse from *Śrīmad-Bhāgavatam* stating that even if born in a family of dog-eaters, whoever constantly chants the holy name of Kṛṣṇa is greater than the most exalted *brāhmaṇa*.

At the house of Vallabha Bhaṭṭa, Caitanya Mahāprabhu met an enlightened Vaiṣṇava scholar named Raghupati Upādhyāya, with whom He discussed topics of Kṛṣṇa. Raghupati Upādhyāya recited a verse he had composed in glorification of Kṛṣṇa, upon hearing which Lord Caitanya became overwhelmed with ecstatic love:

> Those who are afraid of material existence worship Vedic literature, some worship the corollaries of Vedic literature, and others worship *Mahābhārata*. As far as I am concerned, I worship Mahārāja Nanda, the father of Kṛṣṇa, in whose courtyard the Supreme Personality of Godhead, the Absolute Truth, is playing.

Being questioned by Gaurāṅga, Raghupati Upādhyāya averred that of all forms of the Personality of Godhead, Śyāmasundara is best, of all abodes of Śyāmasundara, Mathurā is best, of all ages of Śyāmasundara, *kiśora* (youth) is best, and of all moods in which Śyāmasundara can be worshiped, *mādhurya-rasa* (sweet conjugal relationship) is best.

Back in Prayāga, Lord Caitanya sat with Rūpa Gosvāmī in a quiet spot on the bank of the Gaṅgā and for ten days continuously instructed him in the science of Kṛṣṇa consciousness so that in the future he could write many books about devotional service, including such confidential topics as the relationship between Kṛṣṇa and Śrīmatī Rādhārāṇī. After empowering Rūpa Gosvāmī with the spiritual potency required to write authoritatively about Kṛṣṇa, Caitanya Mahāprabhu prepared to leave for Varanasi. Unable to bear the Lord's separation, Rūpa Gosvāmī asked for permission to follow Him, but Gaurāṅga did not grant it. "Your duty is to execute My order," He instructed. "You have come near Vṛndāvana, so now you should go there. Later you can travel to Purī, where we will meet again." After embracing Rūpa Gosvāmī, Śrī Caitanya Mahāprabhu got into a boat. Rūpa Gosvāmī fainted and fell down on the spot. Thereafter he and his brother Anupama left for Vṛndāvana.

The night before Mahāprabhu arrived at Varanasi, Candraśekhara dreamt that the Lord had visited his home. So early the next morning he went to meet Gaurāṅga at the city gate. Although Candraśekhara belonged to the *śūdra* caste, the Lord agreed to stay with him. Social custom enjoined sannyasis to repose either in an ashram, the home of a *brāhmaṇa*, or under a tree—but certainly not with a *śūdra*, whose association and very touch was considered contaminating. Nonetheless, Lord Caitanya wanted to demonstrate how *bhakti* is not subject to caste considerations. Defying rigid tradition, Mahāprabhu considered glorious anyone who worshiped Kṛṣṇa, and anyone seriously engaged in devotional service to the Supreme Lord, even if otherwise regarded lowborn, He regarded as more exalted than a high-born *brāhmaṇa* devoid of Kṛṣṇa consciousness. Indeed, among Lord Caitanya's foremost followers were Rūpa and Sanātana, previously considered Muslims, and Haridāsa Ṭhākura, extolled as *nāmācārya* (instructor of the holy name) even though from a Muslim background.

One day while sitting in the house of Candraśekhara, Lord Caitanya suddenly declared, "There is a Vaiṣṇava waiting outside. Please bring him in." Candraśekhara went out but saw only a bearded, dirty-looking

Muslim mendicant. "There's no Vaiṣṇava at the door," Candraśekhara reported. "Is there anybody at all?" Lord Caitanya inquired. "Yes, a Muslim fakir." Hearing this, Lord Caitanya ran out of the house and embraced the mendicant, and both of them shed tears of ecstasy while Candraśekhara looked on in astonishment. The apparent fakir was Sanātana Gosvāmī, who had fled in disguise from the imprisonment of the Muslim king of Bengal.

"My dear Lord, please do not touch me," Sanātana pleaded. "I am fallen and unworthy of Your embrace." The Lord replied, "My dear Sanātana, saints of your caliber can purify even places of pilgrimage. I am touching you just to purify Myself. Kṛṣṇa has saved you from the deepest hell. He is an ocean of mercy and His activities are unfathomable." Sanātana replied, "I do not know

Mahāprabhu embraces Sanātana

who Kṛṣṇa is. As far as I am concerned, it is Your mercy that released me from prison."

Lord Caitanya spent a further two months in Varanasi, instructing Sanātana Gosvāmī in the science of devotional service and illuminating him with the deepest and most sublime truths of Vedic wisdom. He explained the constitutional position of the living entity as an eternal servant of Kṛṣṇa, the three features of the absolute truth—Brahman, Paramātmā, and Bhagavān—the nature of the material and spiritual worlds, and the characteristics of a fully realized soul. He described the superiority of *bhakti* to the paths of philosophical speculation and yogic mysticism, the many expansions and forms of the Supreme Personality of Godhead, His avatars within the material world, and the process of devotional service. He revealed that to worship Lord Śrī Kṛṣṇa in Vṛndāvana is the highest platform of spiritual understanding and

Instructing Sanātana Gosvāmī in the science of devotional service

told of the different periods of Kṛṣṇa's age, Kṛṣṇa's various pastimes within those periods, and how Kṛṣṇa attained His permanent form upon reaching full youth. He also enlightened Sanātana regarding esoteric knowledge of spiritual ecstasy experienced by souls who have achieved pure love for Kṛṣṇa. The sweetness and grandeur of these teachings by the Lord were like an ocean overflooding the mind of Sanātana Gosvāmī.

Mahāprabhu's public dancing and chanting of the Hare Kṛṣṇa *mahā-mantra* shocked the many sannyasis of Varanasi. As Māyāvādīs, they believed that the absolute truth has no form, eyes, legs, ears, or personality and that merely by adopting *sannyāsa* a man becomes God. Proudly and absurdly considering themselves God, the foolish Māyāvādīs dared to criticize Lord Caitanya's *saṅkīrtana* as unsuitable for a sannyasi. But Mahāprabhu did not care for them. Avoiding their company He simply continued chanting and dancing.

The devotees of Lord Caitanya in Varanasi—Tapana Miśra, Candraśekhara, and one Maharashtrian *brāhmaṇa*—were deeply unhappy to hear the Māyāvādī sannyasis' endless criticism. One day the

Maharashtrian *brāhmaṇa* decided to invite Mahāprabhu and all the sannyasis of Varanasi for lunch. His idea was that if the Māyāvādīs were to see the divine characteristics of Śrī Caitanya Mahāprabhu, they would accept Him as the Supreme Personality of Godhead. Understanding the *brāhmaṇa's* intention and the distress of His devotees, Gaurāṅga accepted the invitation.

When on the next day Lord Caitanya entered the house of this *brāhmaṇa*, the Māyāvādī sannyasis were already there. As per the custom, upon arriving Mahāprabhu washed His feet. But then He sat down in the very spot where others had washed their feet. "Why are You sitting in a dirty place?" inquired Prakāśānanda Sarasvatī, the leader of the Māyāvādīs, who had sixty thousand disciples. Lord Caitanya replied, "My dear sir, I am not from such an advanced order of *sannyāsa* as you are, and hence not fit to sit with you." Appreciating Gaurāṅga's humility, Prakāśānanda clasped His hand and brought Him to sit among the other sannyasis. Lord Caitanya then demonstrated a bodily effulgence which clearly revealed Him to be the Supreme Personality of Godhead.

Thus the Māyāvādī sannyasis, who falsely considered themselves to be Nārāyaṇa, recognized Mahāprabhu as actually Nārāyaṇa.

Although moved by Lord Caitanya's humility and display of opulence, Prakāśānanda Sarasvatī still wanted to challenge Him on philosophical grounds. "I understand that Your name is Śrī Kṛṣṇa Caitanya and You belong to our *sampradāya*," he began. "So why are You avoiding our association? Why do You indulge in chanting and dancing in the company of fanatics? This is improper for a sannyasi, who is supposed to perform austerities, meditate, and study *Vedānta-sūtra*. You look as brilliant as Nārāyaṇa Himself. Will You kindly explain why You have adopted the behavior of low-class people?"

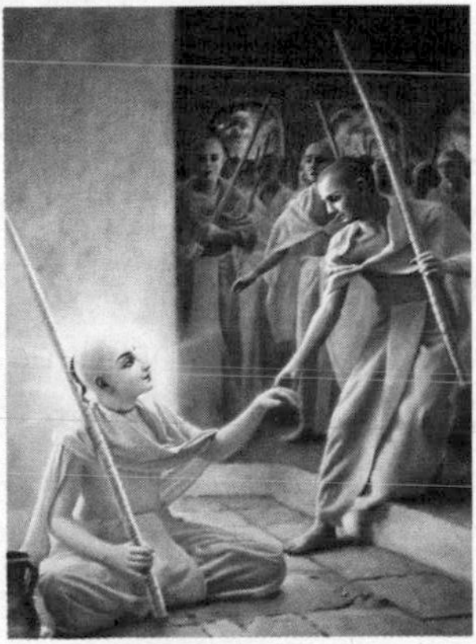

Prakāśānanda appreciates Gaurāṅga's humility

Mahāprabhu replied, "Considering Me a fool, My spiritual master forbade me to study Vedānta. He ordered Me to chant the holy name of Kṛṣṇa incessantly, perform *saṅkīrtana* in the association of devotees, and preach to all people the value of *kṛṣṇa-nāma*. The holy name of Kṛṣṇa is the essence of all Vedic hymns. Simply by chanting Kṛṣṇa's name one becomes free from material existence and attains the lotus feet of the Lord. In this Age of Kali the chanting of the holy name of Kṛṣṇa is the only way to make spiritual progress. But anyway, I can say something about *Vedānta*. *Vedānta* consists of words spoken by Lord Nārāyaṇa in His form of Vyāsadeva. These words are meant to be understood as they are, yet Śrīpāda Śaṅkarācārya has given indirect meanings to them. Whoever hears his explanations becomes spiritually ruined. Yet Śaṅkarācārya is an avatar of Lord Śiva and thus not at fault. He acted on the order of the Supreme Personality of Godhead to cover the real purpose of the Vedas and bewilder atheists in the Age of Kali."

Discussion with Prakāśānanda Sarasvatī

After Lord Caitanya explained at length the real meaning of *Vedānta*, the Māyāvādī sannyasis surrendered at His lotus feet, admitting, "You are Vedic knowledge personified and directly Nārāyaṇa Himself. Please forgive the offenses we previously committed by criticizing You." The Lord pardoned them and instructed them to chant Hare Kṛṣṇa.

The conversion of Prakāśānanda Sarasvatī and his followers was a significant victory for Mahāprabhu, who when leaving Varanasi joked, "I came here to sell some goods, but finding no customers I gave them away for free." In other words, He had come to offer Kṛṣṇa consciousness, but despite finding no takers among the Māyāvādīs He nonetheless found a way to give them His message.

Chapter Eight

Pastimes with Devotees in Purī

Śrī Caitanya Mahāprabhu was eager to return to Purī. Just before leaving Varanasi He instructed Sanātana Gosvāmī to join Rūpa and Anupama in Vṛndāvana and thereat write a book on rules of conduct for Vaiṣṇavas, relocate and renovate lost places of Kṛṣṇa's pastimes in the Vṛndāvana area, install deities of Kṛṣṇa in different sites, dedicate his life to spreading Kṛṣṇa consciousness, and give shelter to and maintain Lord Caitanya's devotees who visit Vṛndāvana.

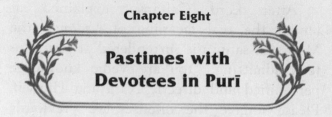

In Purī, Mahāprabhu met Raghunātha dāsa, who was from an extraordinarily wealthy family of landowners. In his childhood he had served Haridāsa Ṭhākura and thus developed both a taste for chanting the holy names of Kṛṣṇa and an overwhelming desire to join Lord Caitanya. Although pious and dedicated to Mahāprabhu, Raghunātha's parents did not want their son to leave. They married him to a ravishing young girl, expecting that this would tie him to materialistic life. But it did not.

After Gaurāṅga took *sannyāsa*, Raghunātha dāsa went to meet Him in Shantipur to express his desire to renounce family life. "Don't be a crazy fellow," the Lord replied. "For now, remain at home and behave like an ordinary materially attached householder, while internally always thinking of Kṛṣṇa. Eventually you will get the chance to fully serve Him." So Raghunātha dāsa returned and for one year discharged his duties like an expert business manager. The next year he again decided to depart for Purī. Yet after fleeing a considerable distance he was captured by his father's men and dragged back. This became a pattern. Again and again Raghunātha would run away, and again and again his father would send men to bring him back.

One day in the village known as Pānihāṭi, Raghunātha dāsa met Nityānanda Prabhu, who ordered him to immediately arrange a huge festival. Raghunātha dāsa fed the thousands present with chipped-rice and yogurt, and many other delectable foods. Afterward Raghunātha dāsa prayed to Lord Nityānanda

Pānihāṭi festival

for His blessings. "No one can attain shelter of Śrī Caitanya Mahāprabhu without Your mercy," he pleaded. "But if You are merciful, even the lowest of men can gain the shelter of His lotus feet."

"My dear Raghunātha," Lord Nityānanda replied, "Mahāprabhu will soon accept you and place you under the charge of His secretary Svarūpa Dāmodara. Thus you will become one of the Lord's most confidential servants." The meeting of Raghunātha dāsa with Lord Nityānanda illustrates that one cannot obtain Lord Caitanya's shelter without first receiving the mercy of Lord Nityānanda.

Soon after returning home, Raghunātha dāsa got a chance to escape. Walking fifty kilometers per day along little-used paths, he reached Purī in twelve days. Mahāprabhu entrusted him to Svarūpa Dāmodara after giving him the following instructions: "Do not talk like common people or listen to their gossip. Do not eat palatable food or dress opulently. Do not expect honor, but offer all respect to others. Always chant the holy name of Lord Kṛṣṇa, and within your mind serve Rādhā-Kṛṣṇa in Vṛndāvana."

Although Raghunātha dāsa had come from a most affluent background, his life in Purī was a model of extreme renunciation. For the first five days he took *prasāda* sent by Lord Caitanya through His personal servant Govinda. But from the sixth day, following the custom of poverty-stricken Vaiṣṇavas he would beg alms each evening at the temple gate. After some time he considered that to depend upon contributions from others was similar to prostitution, so he should instead fill his belly with whatever was provided once daily at the charity booth. After a while he stopped eating there and simply collected rotten rice *prasāda* that even the cows shunned. He would thoroughly wash the putrid grains with ample water and eat the hard inner portion along with salt. Pleased with Raghunātha dāsa's self-abnegation Mahāprabhu came to see him and asked, "What delicious items are you enjoying? Why don't you give some to Me?" He snatched a handful of rice and upon eating it declared, "I have never tasted such wonderful *prasāda!*"

Throughout his life Raghunātha dāsa never succumbed to sense indulgence. He wore only a torn loincloth and a patchwork shawl. His observance of regulative principles was so fixed as to be compared with the lines on a rock. Highly satisfied with Raghunātha dāsa, Lord Caitanya gave him a *śīlā* (stone) from Govardhana Hill and a small garland of *guñjā* (a red and black berry native to Vṛndāvana). The Lord directed Raghunātha dāsa to worship the stone, which Raghunātha dāsa saw as nondifferent from Kṛṣṇa. Considering how he had received the *govardhana-śilā* directly from the hands of Śrī Caitanya Mahāprabhu, Raghunātha dāsa was always overflooded with ecstatic love.

Raghunātha's renunciation pleases Mahāprabhu

Śivānanda Sena would lead the party of Bengali devotees whenever it traveled to Orissa. Along the route he would organize *prasāda* and lodgings, make arrangements to cross the rivers by boat, and pay the tax men at toll booths. One time while the devotees were walking to Purī continuously chanting Hare Kṛṣṇa, Hare Kṛṣṇa, Kṛṣṇa Kṛṣṇa, Hare Hare/ Hare Rāma, Hare Rāma, Rāma Rāma, Hare Hare, a dog followed them. Śivānanda Sena considered that since it had joined a party of Vaiṣṇavas, the dog must also be a Vaiṣṇava. So every day he arranged for it to be fed.

At one toll booth the collector harassed Śivānanda Sena. "The members of my party are tired and hungry," Śivānanda petitioned him. "Let them pass and I will sort things out with you." The toll collector agreed, so everyone went ahead except Śivānanda. When later in the evening Śivānanda finally caught up, he asked if all had taken *prasāda*, and the devotees replied that they had. He then inquired about the dog. It had not been given *prasāda* and no one could find him. Since his duty was to look after everyone but he had failed to care for the dog, Śivānanda considered that he had committed an offense and thus decided to fast.

When the party reached Purī and Śivānanda approached Caitanya Mahāprabhu, he saw Him throwing *prasāda* to that same dog, who was catching it in his mouth. "Chant

Hare Kṛṣṇa!" Gaurāṅga told the dog—who immediately started to chant. Seeing this, Śivānanda offered obeisances to the dog. The next day it was no longer to be seen, for by the blessings of Caitanya Mahāprabhu the soul inhabiting that body had gone back to Godhead. Because the living entity in that condemned form of a dog had somehow attained the kind attention of a great Vaiṣṇava, Gaurāṅga had delivered him.

Bhagavān Ācārya, a devotee of Mahāprabhu in Purī, was by nature exceedingly liberal. But Svarūpa Dāmodara, who was strict and could not tolerate anything contrary to the principles of pure devotional service, sometimes questioned Bhagavān Ācārya's sagacity. Once Bhagavān Ācārya's younger brother Gopāla came to visit him. By studying in Varanasi Gopāla had become adept in describing *Vedānta-sūtra* according to Śaṅkarācārya's commentary, which absurdly attempts to equate the *jīva* (infinitesimal living entity) with Bhagavān, the Supreme Personality of Godhead. Impressed with his brother's apparent scriptural expertise, Bhagavān Ācārya invited Svarūpa Dāmodara to listen to Gopāla's explanations. But Svarūpa Dāmodara angrily told Bhagavān

Ācārya that he had lost his sense of propriety and warned him not to associate with Māyāvādīs, be they even his own kin, because by hearing Māyāvāda commentaries even celebrated devotees can fall from the spiritual path. Bhagavān Ācārya thus sent Gopāla away and gave up all connection with him.

Another time Bhagavān Ācārya invited Mahāprabhu to his home for lunch. Wanting to offer the Lord the best rice available, he sent Choṭa Haridāsa to beg some from the house of Mādhavī devī, an elderly renounced lady devotee of the Lord.* While taking his meal Gaurāṅga praised the quality of the rice and inquired from where it had come. Bhagavān Ācārya replied that Mādhavī devī had supplied it. Mahāprabhu then asked who had begged the rice from Mādhavī devī, and Bhagavān Ācārya said Choṭa Haridāsa.

After finishing *prasāda* the Lord instructed His servant Govinda to henceforth prohibit Choṭa Haridāsa from seeing Him. The devotees present were surprised, for Choṭa Haridāsa was one of Mahāprabhu's intimate celibate associates and his singing was highly appreciated by the Lord. Naturally they asked

* Choṭa Haridāsa should not be confused with Haridāsa Ṭhākura.

Gaurāṅga to explain what offense Choṭa Haridāsa had committed. The Lord said He could not tolerate lustful desire within a renunciant. He knew that at Mādhavī devī's residence Choṭa Haridāsa had seen a young woman, whereupon lust had awakened in his heart.

After Haridāsa had fasted for three days the devotees petitioned Caitanya Mahāprabhu to forgive his minor offense and allow him back. Unexpectedly, Gaurāṅga warned them to stop raising this matter lest He not only continue to disregard Haridāsa, but leave Purī forever. The devotees became afraid and thus no longer mentioned Haridāsa to Mahāprabhu. On their advice Haridāsa broke his fast and simply yearned for his Lord to recall him. For an entire year, he would wait on the road upon which Gaurāṅga walked to the temple of Lord Jagannātha, and from a long distance take *darśana* of Mahāprabhu and offer obeisances. But the Lord did not ask for him. Finally Haridāsa went to Prayāga and drowned himself.

Shortly afterward, one night while walking along the beach at Purī, Svarūpa Dāmodara and accompanying devotees heard beautiful singing from the sky. It sounded just like Haridāsa, so the devotees speculated that in frustration he had committed suicide and become a ghost. But Svarūpa Dāmodara protested that an intimate associate of Lord Caitanya could not become a ghost, so Haridāsa must have attained a transcendental body. Factually this was correct. Unseen by others, Haridāsa would come to sing for Mahāprabhu, who again accepted him and his singing. The Lord's apparently harsh treatment of Haridāsa indicated His resolve that any person who assumes the role of a sadhu should not hypocritically retain material desires.

Upon Gaurahari's request, Sanātana Gosvāmī came from Vṛndāvana to visit Him in Purī. Along the way, in Jharkhand forest, Sanātana bathed in contaminated water and thus contracted a disease which made his body itch with pus-oozing sores. In Purī, Sanātana stayed with Haridāsa Ṭhākura, whom Mahāprabhu visited daily. Every day the Lord would embrace Sanātana, against his desire, for Sanātana considered himself lowly and fallen and certainly did not want pus from his body to touch Mahāprabhu. Sanātana unhappily pondered, "I took birth in this sacred land of India, but due to this sick and useless body could render no service. Therefore, in the upcoming Ratha-yātrā I will relinquish it under the wheel of Jagannātha's cart."

Being present in everyone's heart, Lord Caitanya could understand Sanātana's intention and asked him, "What kind of gentleman are you? Since you have already surrendered your life to Me, your body is My property. You have no right to destroy it." Sanātana explained how he was unhappy at the Lord's embracing him and thus causing him to commit offenses. Mahāprabhu averred that because Sanātana was such a great devotee He was hugging him for His own purification. He then again clasped Sanātana, whereupon the disease and all sores left his body.

Mahāprabhu forbids Sanātana from relinquishing his body

"I have many important tasks to perform in Vṛndāvana and Mathurā," the Lord told

Sanātana, "but because I promised My mother that I would stay in Purī, I have to accomplish them through your body. Do not destroy it." After Gaurāṅga left, Haridāsa Ṭhākura also embraced Sanātana Gosvāmī. "You are the most fortunate person!" he exclaimed. "Caitanya Mahāprabhu has accepted your body as His own personal property, and on His behalf has deputed you to perform vital services in the holy land of Mathurā."

Pradyumna Miśra, a relative of Mahāprabhu's, once came to hear *kṛṣṇa-kathā* from the Lord, who instead directed him to approach Rāmānanda Rāya.* But Rāmānanda was not at home when Pradyumna Miśra arrived. After a long time Rāmānanda finally returned, whereupon he apologized for not having been informed of Pradyumna's coming, and explained how he had been busy dressing some *deva-dāsīs* and teaching them the art of dancing for the pleasure of Lord Jagannātha.† Because it was already late, Pradyumna Miśra returned to his residence without disclosing the purpose of his call.

---

* *Kṛṣṇa-kathā*—discussion of topics of Kṛṣṇa.

† *Deva-dāsīs*—females who dance, sing, and enact dramas for the pleasure of the residing deity of a temple.

When Mahāprabhu later inquired from him about his visit to Rāmānanda Rāya, Pradyumna Miśra expressed surprise at how a respectable gentleman could be dressing *deva-dāsīs* with his own hands. Lord Caitanya asserted that such was impossible for everyone except Rāmānanda Rāya. "He hasn't even the slightest lustful desire in his heart. While dressing the *deva-dāsīs* he simply thinks how to array them attractively so that their performance will please Lord Jagannātha." So the next day Pradyumna Miśra returned to Rāmānanda Rāya and heard such wonderful *kṛṣṇa-kathā* from him that his heart was completely satisfied.

A Bengali poet had composed a drama comparing Lord Jagannātha and Lord Caitanya, which all the devotees appreciated and wanted Mahāprabhu to hear. But the standing rule was that no literary work could be presented to Gaurāṅga unless Svarūpa Dāmodara had first assessed it, because Gaurāṅga disliked listening to any composition that was even slightly divergent from the principles of pure devotional service. Upon hearing the introductory verses, Svarūpa Dāmodara detected philosophical misconceptions. Consequently he advised the poet to hear *Śrīmad-Bhāgavatam* from a pure devotee of Kṛṣṇa and take full shelter of Caitanya Mahāprabhu; in this way he would be able to obtain the Lord's mercy and actually understand the philosophy of Kṛṣṇa consciousness, and only thereby gain the qualification to write Kṛṣṇa conscious literature.

Every night in Purī Mahāprabhu performed *saṅkīrtana* with His associates. Thousands of people would participate, including higher beings from all over the universe. Disguised as pilgrims, they would come for *darśana* of their Lord. Even Prahlāda Mahārāja, Bali Mahārāja, Vyāsadeva, Śukadeva Gosvāmī, and other reputed personages came to visit Gaurāṅga. Upon seeing Him they became unconscious in ecstatic love for Kṛṣṇa.

Mahārāja Pratāparudra had arranged for Gaurahari's men to get as much Jagannātha-*prasāda* as they wanted. They used to chant Hare Kṛṣṇa with thousands of men for at least four hours every night, and when everyone became tired the devotees would profusely distribute *prasāda*. In this way all tasted the bliss of Mahāprabhu's *saṅkīrtana* movement—

simply by chanting, dancing, and relishing *prasāda*.

Once after visiting the Jagannātha temple early in the morning, Lord Caitanya and His accompanying devotees began *kīrtana*. Mahāprabhu started jumping high. His teeth loosened and His body trembled and became covered with eruptions. The *kīrtana* grew so intense, and their absorption in chanting the holy name of Kṛṣṇa so complete, that forgetting their minds, bodies, homes, and all else, they experienced nothing except the name of Kṛṣṇa.

When in mid-afternoon the *kīrtana* was still continuing and the devotees exhausted from more than ten hours of chanting and dancing, Nityānanda Prabhu devised a way to stop the *kīrtana* without shocking Mahāprabhu, who was still totally rapt in the transcendental nectar of the holy names. One by one Nityānanda stopped the devotees who were singing, leaving only Svarūpa Dāmodara chanting softly. Mahāprabhu then came to external consciousness and asked why the *saṅkīrtana* had ended. Nityānanda replied that it was now afternoon yet Mahāprabhu had not performed His midday duties or taken *prasāda*.

Each day after Mahāprabhu had accepted *prasāda* at noon, Govinda would massage Him for a few minutes. After Gaurāṅga had fallen asleep, Govinda would honor His *mahā-prasāda* remnants. But on the day of the extended *kīrtana* Gaurahari was so exhausted that on returning to His room He collapsed in the doorway. When asked to move slightly aside so that Govinda could enter to massage Him, Mahāprabhu replied, "I am too tired to move. Do whatever you like." So Govinda lay his top cloth over the Lord's body, offered obeisances, crossed over Him, and began massaging Him. Upon awaking from rest and seeing Govinda still sitting nearby, Gaurāṅga somewhat angrily asked why he had not yet taken *prasāda*. Govinda answered that he had not wanted to cross over the Lord's body. "So how did you come inside?" Mahāprabhu inquired. Govinda did not reply but simply thought, "For the

Govinda crosses over the Lord

sake of serving my master I may commit an offense and go to hell, yet for my own sense gratification I don't want to even dream of making the slightest shadow of an offense."

One time upon bringing Jagannātha-*prasāda* to Haridāsa Ṭhākura, Govinda found him lying down, apparently ill, chanting *japa* slowly. "What is wrong?" Govinda asked. "I cannot finish my rounds," Haridāsa replied. Govinda left the *prasāda,* and returning to Mahāprabhu, reported Haridāsa's condition to Him.

The next day Lord Caitanya came and asked about his health Haridāsa again stated, "My disease is inability to finish my quota of *japa.*" Mahāprabhu replied, "Now you are old, and already a perfect devotee, so you do not need to chant so many rounds." Haridāsa submitted, "My dear Lord, kindly hear my real desire. I know You will not stay in this world much longer, and I cannot bear to live here without You. Please allow me to leave before You." Gaurāṅga contended, "Haridāsa, you are such an exalted personality that it will be a great detriment to the world if you depart." "I am insignificant," Haridāsa replied. "If an ant dies, what is the loss for anyone? If I go, what will be the harm? I want to quit this earthly plane while seeing Your moonlike face."

On the following day, Mahāprabhu came with His associates and described the qualities and character of Haridāsa. The devotees were enthralled to hear of the extraordinary activities Haridāsa had performed throughout his life, having calmly continued chanting the holy names with all tolerance and humility even amidst exacting difficulties. Not only had he chanted the holy name incessantly, but had also preached far and wide the glories of the holy name.

Gaurāṅga started *kīrtana* and Haridāsa knelt before Him. As the tempo increased, Haridāsa gazed at the lotus face of his beloved Lord, and uttering "Śrī Kṛṣṇa Caitanya" again and again, he quit this world. Mahāprabhu took Haridāsa's body in His arms and danced. Then He and the devotees

Haridāsa Ṭhākura's disappearance festival

bathed that transcendental form in the sea and prepared a shrine for it on the beach. "By the touch of Haridāsa's glorious body, this sea has now become a *mahā-tīrtha* (great holy place)," He declared. Desiring to conduct a memorable festival in honor of Haridāsa Ṭhākura's departure, the Lord personally begged Jagannātha-*prasāda* from all the shopkeepers, and blessed all present at the festival to attain love for God.

Every year the devotees from Bengal were highly reluctant to leave Purī after Cāturmāsya, and likewise Mahāprabhu was reluctant to let them go. Each year they would postpone their departure for a few days, and then again for some more days, until eventually they dragged themselves onto the path leading to Bengal. One time as they were setting off Lord Caitanya said, "Just for My sake all of you undergo severe hardships to come here. Advaita Ācārya is now old but still comes, and Nityānanda, unable to bear separation from Me, keeps breaking My order that He remain preaching in Bengal. All of you are so affectionate to Me, yet I have nothing to offer you in return. I am a poor sannyasi with no possession other than this body. Therefore I simply give Myself to you in repayment for your love." Hearing these love-laden words, the devotees' hearts melted and torrents of tears flowed from their eyes. Caitanya Mahāprabhu embraced all His devotees, who eventually departed to tend to their household duties.

Jagadānanda Paṇḍita had been an intimate associate of Gaurāṅga's since childhood. He had accompanied Lord Caitanya to Purī upon His taking *sannyāsa* and remained with Him ever since. In *kṛṣṇa-līlā* Jagadānanda is Satyabhāma, one of Kṛṣṇa's principal queens. Just as Satyabhāma was famous for her quarrels of love with Kṛṣṇa, Jagadānanda was known to often become angry with Caitanya Mahāprabhu. And the Lord accepted that sentiment.

One time Mahāprabhu sent Jagadānanda to Bengal to bring news of His activities to His mother. While there, Jagadānanda collected much sandalwood and with immense labor and difficulty extracted its oil, intending to use it for massaging Mahāprabhu's head. Taking utmost care not to spill even a drop, Jagadānanda brought the valuable oil back to Purī in a big pot and, with great happiness presented it to Gaurahari. But the Lord refused it, saying, "I am a sannyasi. If I use sweet-scented oil, people will think I am keeping women. Your endeavor will be fruitful if the oil is burned in the lamps of the Jagannātha temple."

Incensed, Jagadānanda grabbed the pot of sandalwood oil, smashed it in the courtyard, and returned to his residence. He bolted the door and simply lay on his bed for three days, fasting. On the fourth day Caitanya Mahāprabhu came and gently asked, "Jagadānanda, will you please cook for Me today?" Forgetting his anger, Jagadānanda arose, bathed, and cooked a huge *prasāda* feast for the Lord. He also served the *prasāda*, constantly refilling Gaurāṅga's plate, insisting that He take more and more. The Lord kept on eating, fearing that if He stopped, Jagadānanda would again become upset and

Angry Jagadānanda smashes the pot

continue fasting. Finally He told Jagadānanda that He had eaten ten times more than usual and begged him also to take *prasāda*.

Chapter Nine

The Final Years

For the last eighteen years of His manifest presence on earth, Lord Caitanya remained in Purī, increasingly absorbed in the bittersweet ecstasy of separation from Kṛṣṇa. In daytime, various activities would somewhat divert His mind, but at night He suffered heart-rending separation from Kṛṣṇa, just as Rādhārāṇī had experienced after Kṛṣṇa left Vṛndāvana for Mathurā.

During this period the Lord sometimes manifested external consciousness, wherein He would speak and relate to people according to worldly standards of normalcy, at other times became so immersed in thoughts of Kṛṣṇa as to be entirely unaware of the world around Him, not even knowing if it was day or night, and sometimes was in marginal consciousness. Svarūpa Dāmodara, Rāmānanda Rāya, and Govinda were His constant companions. At night He would clasp the necks of Rāmānanda

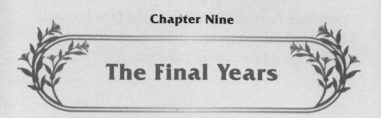

Lord Caitanya in ecstasy

Rāya and Svarūpa Dāmodara and in the mood of Rādhārāṇī lament, "Alas! Alas! My dearmost friend Śrī Kṛṣṇa has left for Mathurā, plunging Me into an ocean of grief. How can I live without Him? Where shall I go to find My beloved Kṛṣṇa?" Svarūpa Dāmodara and Rāmānanda Rāya would enhance the Lord's mood of devotion by singing songs about Kṛṣṇa.

One day while going toward the sea for His noontime bath, Mahāprabhu saw a large sand dune. Mistaking it to be Govardhana Hill, He ran toward it in divine madness, reciting a verse the *gopīs* had sung in glorification of Govardhana:

> Of all the devotees, this Govardhana Hill is the best. O My friends, this hill supplies Kṛṣṇa and Balarāma and Their calves, cows, and cowherd friends with all kinds of necessities—

drinking water, soft grass, caves, fruits, flowers, and vegetables. Thus Govardhana Hill offers respect to the Lord and appears jubilant upon being touched by the lotus feet of Kṛṣṇa and Balarāma.

Glorifying Govardhana in ecstasy

His voice choked up and with tears incessantly running down His cheeks, Caitanya Mahāprabhu ran as swiftly as the wind while His devotees chased after Him. Blood oozed from His pores and His body turned white. Trembling like ocean waves, He crashed to the ground, unconscious. The devotees were devastated.

Govinda sprinkled Mahāprabhu's body with water from His pot, while Svarūpa Dāmodara and the other devotees chanted "Kṛṣṇa! Kṛṣṇa!" in His ears. Eventually Gaurāṅga jumped up, chanting "Hari! Hari!" The devotees were both relieved and delighted to see Him return to external consciousness. But still only semi-conscious, and weeping bitterly in separation from Kṛṣṇa, Caitanya Mahāprabhu asked painfully of Svarūpa Dāmodara, "Why have you brought Me back here? I was seeing Kṛṣṇa with Rādhārāṇī and the *gopīs* on Govardhana Hill. Why have you taken Me from there?"

One night Mahāprabhu saw the moonlight glittering on the ocean. Mistaking the sea for the Yamunā, He ran and jumped in. Lost in ecstasy, He floated several kilometers north to the place known as Konark. When the devotees discovered that Lord Caitanya was gone, they searched up and down the beach, but unable to find Him even by dawn they feared that He had left the world. Early in the morning they reached Konark, where they met a frightened fisherman chanting the name of Nṛsiṁhadeva. Sensing that he might have some clue about Mahāprabhu's whereabouts, Svarūpa Dāmodara asked him why he looked so afraid.

Mahāprabhu crashes to the ground unconscious

The fisherman replied, "Last night I caught a peculiar ghost in my net. Its limbs were separated from its body. When I go fishing at night I chant the name of Nṛsiṁhadeva to protect me from ghosts, but this one was so unusual that the more I chanted the name of Nṛsiṁhadeva, the more powerful He became." Understanding the whole situation, Svarūpa Dāmodara told him, "Don't worry, I know how to get rid of ghosts." He then chanted some mantras, placed his hand on the fisherman's head, slapped him three times, and pronounced, "Now the ghost has gone away. Don't be afraid." Having thus pacified the fisherman, Svarūpa Dāmodara explained, "The person you think is a ghost is actually the Supreme Personality of Godhead, Śrī Kṛṣṇa Caitanya Mahāprabhu. Now that your fear has gone and your mind is peaceful, please show me where He is."

Mahāprabhu in the fisherman's net

The fisherman led the devotees to his nets, whereat they found their master lying unconscious and covered with sand. His body was stretched, His bones displaced, and His skin slack and hanging loose. Replacing His wet loincloth, the devotees cleaned and dried His body, laid Him on a sheet, and chanted Hare Kṛṣṇa in His ears for a long time. All of a sudden Gaurāṅga leapt up with a roar, His limbs reverting to normal.

Still unaware of what was transpiring, Mahāprabhu uttered, "I saw Lord Śrī Kṛṣṇa sporting with Rādhā and the *gopīs* in the water of the Yamunā. My heart was filled with rapture at this pleasant sight, but then you called Me and brought Me here. Where is the Yamunā? Where is Vṛndāvana? Where is Kṛṣṇa? Where are Rādhā and the *gopīs?*" Svarūpa Dāmodara gently led Mahāprabhu back to His residence in Purī and made Him take rest. All the devotees were anxious because Gaurāṅga's mind was lost in thoughts of Kṛṣṇa and it was impossible to predict what He would do next.

One day Svarūpa Dāmodara received an enigmatic message from Advaita Ācārya: "Inform the madman that everyone has become mad like Him. Rice is no longer in demand in the marketplace." Only Caitanya Mahāprabhu and Svarūpa Dāmodara could understand its meaning: Lord Caitanya's appearance had been fulfilled and soon He would depart this world. Svarūpa Dāmodara became somber, and thenceforward Gaurāṅga's ecstasy doubled or tripled every second. Overwhelmed with the madness of separation from Kṛṣṇa, Mahāprabhu could barely sustain His existence. Then one day while performing *saṅkīrtana* with His devotees near the temple of Ṭoṭā-Gopīnātha, He suddenly departed from this world by rushing into the temple and merging into the deity of Gopīnātha.

Unable to bear the separation from their dearmost Lord, most of Mahāprabhu's associates soon also quit the earthly plane. But the Six Gosvāmīs of Vṛndāvana remained behind to continue His work of establishing Kṛṣṇa consciousness.

Epilogue

Lord Caitanya predicted that His movement would spread to every town and village on the planet, and in pursuance of this prophecy His Divine Grace A.C. Bhaktivedanta Swami Prabhupāda founded the International Society for Krishna Consciousness (ISKCON) in 1966 in New York, circled the globe fourteen times, established more than a hundred temples, and thereby made Hare Kṛṣṇa a household phrase before his departure from this world in 1977. ISKCON continues to widely spread the teachings of Śrī Caitanya Mahāprabhu and the chanting of the holy names. Thanks to Śrīla Prabhupāda, to this day the movement begun by Śrī Caitanya Mahāprabhu continues to uplift humanity by freely offering the easiest and best means of attaining spiritual perfection—chanting the *mahā-mantra:*

Hare Kṛṣṇa Hare Kṛṣṇa
Kṛṣṇa Kṛṣṇa Hare Hare
Hare Rāma Hare Rāma
Rāma Rāma Hare Hare

The holy land in which Śrī Caitanya Mahāprabhu appeared, Śrīdhāma Māyāpur, is being developed by ISKCON as a major international pilgrimage site. All are invited to visit whenever possible and avail of the incomparable heart-soothing transcendental atmosphere of Śrīdhāma Māyāpur.

Śrī Māyāpur Candrodaya Temple under construction in Māyāpur

Appendix 1

Lord Caitanya Is the Supreme Personality of Godhead

From time to time the Absolute Truth, the Personality of Godhead, descends into this universe in His original transcendental form. Although under no obligation to do so, He comes for the benefit of the fallen conditioned souls who are struggling in this material world, bereft of knowledge of Him. The Lord's advent is a great mystery to gross materialists. Even most religionists, possessing very limited knowledge of God, doubt how He could personally come to this world. But the Supreme Lord can do whatever He likes, and as detailed in Vedic scriptures, He is pleased to appear on this plane to enact divine pastimes, give succor to His devotees, and uplift the universe. Although one undivided person, He assumes various forms, which are described in scripture and accepted by *ācāryas*. All such spiritual authorities acknowledge that the Supreme Lord, Kṛṣṇa, appeared in His original transcendental form five thousand years ago in Vṛndāvana, near present-day Delhi.

Unfortunately, the modern age has seen a rash of false incarnations. Such impostors speak enticingly and bewilder foolish people into accepting them as God. Such ignoramuses are unaware that genuine avatars must be fully possessed of six opulences: all wealth, supreme power, topmost fame, superlative beauty, complete knowledge, and full renunciation. However, insincere persons want to be cheated, and thus they accept an imitator as God. Hence both the cheaters and the cheated pave their path to hell.

A real avatar is indicated by scriptural references and extraordinary activities impossible even for great yogis to perform. Being actually the Supreme Personality of Godhead Lord Caitanya fulfilled these criteria, as described in *Śrī Caitanya-caritāmṛta.* He was nothing like the cheap imitation so-called avatars. Śrī Caitanya Mahāprabhu was Kṛṣṇa Himself, come in the form of His own devotee to relish the bliss of devotional service and teach others how to worship Him. He did not advertise Himself as the Supreme Lord, for this would have disturbed His mood of being a devotee. Therefore He is considered a covered avatar. As predicted in *Śrīmad-Bhāgavatam*

(7.9.38), the cream of Vedic literature, in Kali-yuga the Supreme Lord appears in a hidden form:

channaḥ kalau yad abhavas tri-yugo 'tha sa tvam

> In the Age of Kali You sometimes appear as a covered avatar. Therefore You are known as Tri-yuga [one who appears in three yugas].

Some scholars interpret this verse to mean that the Lord does not descend into this world in Kali-yuga, but this is inconsistent with His statement in *Bhagavad-gītā* (4.8):

paritrāṇāya sādhūnāṁ
vināśāya ca duṣkṛtām
dharma-saṁsthāpanārthāya
sambhavāmi yuge yuge

> To deliver the pious and annihilate the miscreants, as well as to reestablish the principles of religion, I Myself appear millennium after millennium.

The Lord declares that He appears in every millennium, which indicates His descent also in the Age of Kali. How He appears in this age is described in *Śrīmad-Bhāgavatam* (11.5.32):

kṛṣṇa-varṇaṁ tviṣākṛṣṇaṁ
sāṅgopāṅgāstra-pārṣadam
yajñaiḥ saṅkīrtana-prāyair
yajanti hi su-medhasaḥ

> In the Age of Kali, intelligent persons perform congregational chanting to worship the avatar of Godhead who constantly sings the names of Kṛṣṇa. Although His complexion is not blackish, He is Kṛṣṇa Himself. He is accompanied by His associates, servants, weapons, and confidential companions.

Thus it is understood that the Supreme Lord appears in Kali-yuga to engage in and teach the congregational chanting of His holy names yet remains not directly exposed as the Supreme Lord. This description indicates Lord Caitanya as the avatar of the age.*

At the time of His appearance, Caitanya Mahāprabhu was understood to be the Supreme Lord by great learned scholars such

---

* Many other scriptural evidences of the supreme divinity of Caitanya Mahāprabhu are given in *Glories of Lord Chaitanya* (Kṛṣṇa Institute, Alachua, Florida, USA), a compendium of verses from a variety of sources. Also available at http://www.veda.harekrsna.cz/encyclopedia/caitanya.htm.

as Sārvabhauma Bhaṭṭācārya, Prakāśānanda Sarasvatī, Sanātana Gosvāmī, Rūpa Gosvāmī, Rāmānanda Rāya, and many others. They were not sentimentalists, but knowledgeable and strict followers of Vedic literatures, on which basis they acknowledged Gauraṅga's divinity. They accepted as further evidence Lord Caitanya's extraordinary feats of changing the lives of many fallen sinful people and bestowing upon them the highest love of God. Also, as recorded in His authorized biographies, on several occasions Mahāprabhu revealed to certain intimate devotees His form as Kṛṣṇa.

Further proof of Lord Caitanya's divinity is the present-day spread of Kṛṣṇa consciousness. Many thousands of people throughout the world, although having no background of pious deeds, Vedic culture, or scriptural knowledge, have given up all sinful activities to dedicate their lives in service to Kṛṣṇa. They have become so purified that they are worshiping the deity of Kṛṣṇa and explaining *Śrīmad-Bhāgavatam*. How the most fallen could become the most elevated is possible only by the special mercy of God Himself.

Anyone who accepts Śrī Caitanya Mahāprabhu as the Supreme Personality of Godhead and chants His name together with the names of His associates—*śrī-kṛṣṇa-caitanya prabhu-nityānanda śrī-advaita gadādhara śrīvāsādi-gaura-bhakta-vṛnda*—and also chants the *mahā-mantra* (Hare Kṛṣṇa, Hare Kṛṣṇa, Kṛṣṇa Kṛṣṇa, Hare Hare/ Hare Rāma, Hare Rāma, Rāma Rāma, Hare Hare), will receive the mercy of Lord Caitanya and make rapid progress on the path back to Godhead.

May the powerful flood of Śrī Caitanya's mercy inundate every town, village, home, and heart in the universe! May the most merciful Lord Gaurāṅga be glorified everywhere! May the people of the world chant His divine name and be happy! Mahāprabhu's glories were covered at the time of His appearance, but now they should be preached throughout the globe so that everyone may be benefited. Just as Kṛṣṇa has become well known all over the planet, so should His most merciful avatar Śrī Caitanya Mahāprabhu be known and adored by all.

Appendix 2

Lord Caitanya's Teachings

During the time of Lord Caitanya's pastimes India was a land of philosophy. Each respectable village had its *paṇḍitas*, and at important centers of learning thousands of scholars discoursed and debated Vedic dialectics. As still now, in those days two metaphysical schools were prominent: the Advaita-vāda of Śaṅkarācārya, and the diametrically opposed teachings of the Vaiṣṇavas.

Advaita-vāda seeks to establish that "all is one."* According to its theories there is no supreme controller, ultimate reality is variety-less and formless, perception of form and diversity is simply illusion, and when this illusion is removed the soul sheds its temporary individuality and merges into all-pervading Truth.

Vaiṣṇavas reject these suppositions as inconsistent with logic, common sense, and scriptural conclusions. By opposing the supremacy of the Supreme Personality of

---

* Advaita-vāda—Māyāvāda, monism, impersonalism.

Godhead, Māyāvāda misleads spiritually inclined persons into enviously equating themselves with the Supreme. By thus destroying the attitude of submission to Kṛṣṇa, which is the very basis of *bhakti*, Māyāvāda is the worst aberration in spiritual life. Therefore Vaiṣṇava *ācāryas*, especially Rāmānujācārya and Madhvācārya, strongly attacked Śaṅkarācārya's doctrine, exposed its fallacies, and established that the absolute truth is the personal form of Viṣṇu, or Kṛṣṇa.

Unfortunately, even today impersonalism remains influential due to the wicked mentality of conditioned souls who prefer to deny or avoid God, or consider themselves or an imposter as God, rather than accept the scriptural conclusion that Kṛṣṇa is the Supreme Personality of Godhead and all other living entities His eternal servants.

As befitting a Vaiṣṇava *ācārya*, Lord Caitanya also vigorously opposed the tenets of Śaṅkarācārya. Being the Supreme Personality of Godhead Kṛṣṇa Himself, He perfectly knows the purpose of the Vedas:

vedaiś ca sarvair aham eva vedyo
vedānta-kṛd veda-vid eva cāham

By all the Vedas I am to be known. Indeed I am the compiler of Vedānta and the knower of the Vedas. (*Bhagavad-gītā* 15.15)

With His *acintya-bhedābheda-tattva* (the teaching of simultaneous oneness and difference), Mahāprabhu brought Vaiṣṇava philosophy, and indeed all philosophy, to its ultimate conclusion—that individual souls are one with God in quality but not in quantity, like the relationship between a drop of seawater and the ocean. All of Śrī Caitanya Mahāprabhu's teachings protest the monistic philosophy of the Māyāvāda school and establish as the central point of Kṛṣṇa consciousness that the *jīva* can never be equal to Kṛṣṇa, or Viṣṇu.

Caitanya Mahāprabhu accepted the essence of the philosophies of the four great Vaiṣṇava *ācāryas* who appeared before Him—Rāmānujācārya, Madhvācārya, Viṣṇu Svāmī, and Nimbārka—and adopted two major specialties from each of them. From Madhva He accepted complete defeat of Māyāvāda philosophy, and recognition of the deity form of Kṛṣṇa as an eternal spiritual being. From Rāmānuja He incorporated the concept of

Śrī Rāmānujācārya

Śrī Madhvācārya

Śrī Nimbārkācārya

Śrī Viṣṇu Svāmī

bhakti unpolluted by *karma* and *jñāna*, and the importance of service to devotees. From Viṣṇu Svāmī's teachings He adopted the sentiment of exclusive dependence on Kṛṣṇa, and the path of *rāga-bhakti*. And from Nimbārka He accepted the need to take shelter of Rādhā, and high esteem for the *gopīs*' love for Kṛṣṇa.

Lord Caitanya further taught that as Kṛṣṇa is to be worshiped, so also should His holy abode Vṛndāvana be worshiped. And He accepted *Śrīmad-Bhāgavatam* as the ultimate

Vedic evidence. Yet He went much beyond merely recognizing the existence of God or considering Him a bestower of boons for worldly enjoyment, for He established that the ultimate purpose of life is attainment of love of God, far surpassing ordinary religious rituals, acquisition of wealth, sense gratification, or even liberation from material existence. He declared that conjugal love of God as exemplified by the *gopīs* is the topmost ideal; far from being immoral, the love-saturated dealings between Kṛṣṇa and the *gopīs* are the pinnacle of spiritual exchange. Previous religionists taught service to God with awe and reverence, as befitting the position of the Supreme Being, but Lord Caitanya gave information of a stage of intimate love for God, superseding all formalities.

Śrī Caitanya Mahāprabhu revealed how the Supreme Personality of Godhead Kṛṣṇa sucks the breast of His mother Yaśodā, frolics in the pasturing grounds of Vṛndāvana, and dances with the *gopīs*. Such familiar dealings of the Lord with His devotees are inconceivable to conditioned souls, who are therefore warned neither to deprecate nor imitate them. Yet by Mahāprabhu's mercy, even the most degraded souls of this fallen Age of Kali can become eligible to enter these most confidential pastimes of Kṛṣṇa, speak with Him face to face, and eternally experience the bliss of such loving exchanges.

Lord Caitanya was not simply a philosopher, but a preacher who made the path of love of God available to all. He taught that chanting the holy names of Kṛṣṇa is the most feasible means for self-realization in the modern age, and by this simple method distributed Kṛṣṇa consciousness widely. He predicted that Kṛṣṇa consciousness would spread throughout the world, and ordered His followers to become gurus and preach the message of Kṛṣṇa everywhere.

Caitanya Mahāprabhu did not personally write any books, but instructed his followers, especially the Six Gosvāmīs of Vṛndāvana, to do so—among whom Rūpa, Sanātana, and their nephew Jīva are famous in the Vaiṣṇava and academic communities for their many valuable works. Among Rūpa Gosvāmī's major literary contributions are *Bhakti-rasāmṛta-sindhu*, *Dāna-keli-kaumudī*, *Haṁsadūta*, *Laghu-bhāgavatāmṛta*, *Mathurā-māhātmya*,

Padyāvalī, *Uddhava-sandeśa*, *Ujjvala-nīlamaṇi*, and *Upadeśāmṛta*. His dramas *Lalita-Mādhava* and *Vidagdha-Mādhava* expound the pastimes of Kṛṣṇa in Dvārakā and Vṛndāvana. Sanātana Gosvāmī composed *Bṛhad-bhāgavatāmṛta* and, together with Gopāla Bhaṭṭa Gosvāmī, *Hari-bhakti-vilāsa*. Sanātana Gosvāmī also penned a commentary on the Tenth Canto of *Śrīmad-Bhāgavatam*, called *Daśama-ṭippanī*. Jīva Gosvāmī's *Ṣaṭ-sandarbhas* are six treatises which comprehensively survey Gauḍīya Vaiṣṇava philosophy, and his *Gopāla-campū* is an overview of Kṛṣṇa's pastimes.

Subsequent generations of devotees wrote innumerable books systematically compiling, describing, analyzing, and elaborating the philosophy, practice, and realized stages of Kṛṣṇa consciousness. Thus the teachings of Mahāprabhu were established, maintained, and spread in India up to the modern day. The most recent preeminent representative of Caitanya Mahāprabhu, His Divine Grace A.C. Bhaktivedanta Swami Prabhupāda, contributed more than sixty books lucidly explaining the philosophy of Lord Caitanya in an uncomplicated manner appreciated by scholars and laymen worldwide.

The practical method of God realization propagated by Caitanya Mahāprabhu is that everyone, always and everywhere, chant the names of Kṛṣṇa, especially the *mahā-mantra:*

Hare Kṛṣṇa Hare Kṛṣṇa
Kṛṣṇa Kṛṣṇa Hare Hare
Hare Rāma Hare Rāma
Rāma Rāma Hare Hare

Chanting of these sublime names destroys all sinful effects leading to successive horrors of hellish punishment, birth in animal form, or afflictions such as sickness and poverty. Moreover, this chanting bestows *mukti* (liberation) and, most importantly, pure love of Kṛṣṇa.

Six Gosvāmīs

Appendix 3

Lord Caitanya's Eight Verses of Instruction

Although Lord Caitanya was widely renowned as a scholar in His youth, He left only eight verses, called *Śikṣāṣṭaka.* Those eight verses clearly reveal His mission and precepts. These supremely valuable prayers are translated as follows:

(1) Glory to the *śrī-kṛṣṇa-saṅkīrtana,* which cleanses the heart of all dust accumulated for years and extinguishes the fire of conditional life, of repeated birth and death. This *saṅkīrtana* movement is the prime benediction for humanity at large because it spreads the rays of the benediction moon. It is the life of all transcendental knowledge. It increases the ocean of transcendental bliss, and enables us to fully taste the nectar for which we are always anxious.

(2) O my Lord, Your holy name alone can render all benediction to living beings, and thus You have hundreds and millions of names, like Kṛṣṇa and Govinda. In these

transcendental names You have invested all Your transcendental energies. There are not even hard and fast rules for chanting these names. O my Lord, out of kindness You enable us to easily approach You by Your holy names, but I am so unfortunate that I have no attraction for them.

(3) One should chant the holy name of the Lord in a humble state of mind, thinking oneself lower than straw in the street. One should be more tolerant than a tree, devoid of all sense of false prestige, and ready to offer all respect to others. In such a state of mind one can chant the holy name of the Lord constantly.

(4) O almighty Lord, I have no desire to accumulate wealth, nor do I desire beautiful women, nor any number of followers. I want only Your causeless devotional service, birth after birth.

(5) O son of Mahārāja Nanda [Kṛṣṇa], I am Your eternal servitor, yet somehow or other I have fallen into the ocean of birth and death. Please pick me up from this ocean of death and place me as one of the atoms at Your lotus feet.

(6) O my Lord, when will my eyes be decorated with tears of love flowing constantly when I chant Your holy name? When will my voice choke up and the hairs of my body stand on end at the recitation of Your name?

(7) O Govinda! Feeling Your separation, I am considering a moment to be like twelve

years or more. Tears are flowing from my eyes like torrents of rain, and I am feeling all vacant in the world in Your absence.

(8) I know no one but Kṛṣṇa as my Lord, and He shall remain so even if He handles me roughly by His embrace or makes me brokenhearted by not being present before me. He is completely free to do anything and everything, for He is always my worshipful Lord, unconditionally.

Glossary

Ācārya—(1) spiritual master who by his own example establishes religious truths and standards; (2) title for a teacher or family name for persons descended from teachers.

Ārati—ceremony of worship for the Supreme Lord in His deity manifestation, performed with chanting of mantras and offerings of lamps, fans, flowers, and incense. Also conducted for gurus and demigods.

Balarāma—the brother of Kṛṣṇa, yet simultaneously nondifferent from Him.

Bhakti—process of worshiping Śrī Kṛṣṇa, the Supreme Personality of Godhead, by dedicating one's thoughts, words, and actions to Him in loving submission.

Brahmacārī—celibate student of a spiritual master.

Brahmā—the demigod who is the first created living being and secondary creator of the material universe.

Brāhmaṇa—brahmin.

Darśana—audience of the Supreme Lord or His representative.

Dāsa—(1) male servant; (2) word appended to a name given to a male devotee at the time of initiation, denoting him as a servant of Kṛṣṇa; (3) common family name in Bengal and Orissa.

Dāsī, devī dāsī—(1) female servant; (2) term appended to a name given to a female devotee at the time of initiation, signifying her as a servant of Kṛṣṇa.

Demigods—personalities residing in the higher planets, the principal among whom are assigned by the Supreme Lord to oversee the affairs of the universe and are worshiped for material boons by materialistic followers of Vedic culture.

Ekādaśī—eleventh day of both the waxing and waning moon, on which fasting at least from grains and beans is compulsory for Vaiṣṇavas.

Gaṅgā—Ganges River.

Gāyatrī—mantra recited within the mind by suitably initiated persons at sunrise, midday, and sunset.

Gopīs—Kṛṣṇa's cowherd girlfriends, His most confidential devotees.

Gosvāmī—(1) one who fully controls his senses; (2) title designating a sannyasi.

Govardhana—especially sacred hill within the greater Vṛndāvana area.

Hare Kṛṣṇa mahā-mantra—topmost mantra in all Vedic literature: Hare Kṛṣṇa, Hare Kṛṣṇa, Kṛṣṇa Kṛṣṇa, Hare Hare/ Hare Rāma, Hare Rāma, Rāma Rāma, Hare Hare.

Hari—"He who removes all obstacles to spiritual progress," the Supreme Lord, Śrī Kṛṣṇa.

Impersonalism—*See* **Māyāvāda.**

Jīva—living entity.

ISKCON—International Society for Krishna Consciousness. Founded in 1966 in New York by His Divine Grace A.C. Bhaktivedanta Swami Prabhupāda, it is the principle manifestation of what is popularly known as the Hare Krishna movement.

Jagannātha—"Lord of the universe"; particular deity form of the Lord worshiped principally in Purī, Orissa.

Kali-yuga—the present age of quarrel, hypocrisy, and irreligion, which began somewhat more than five thousand years ago.

Karatālas—small hand cymbals played in accompaniment of *kīrtana.*

Kīrtana—chanting the names and glories of the Supreme Lord. *See also* **Mahā-mantra; Saṅkīrtana.**

Kṛṣṇa—original form of the Supreme Personality of Godhead.

Kṛṣṇa-kathā—discussion of topics about Kṛṣṇa or His pure devotees.

Lakṣmī—goddess of fortune and eternal consort of Lord Nārāyaṇa.

Līlā—transcendental pastime(s) of the Lord and His pure devotees.

Mahābhārata—famous didactic epic and seminal literature at the basis of Indian culture.

Mahā-mantra—*See* **Hare Kṛṣṇa mahā-mantra.**

Mathurā—sacred place where Lord Kṛṣṇa advented, adjacent to Vṛndāvana. Today it is a large town of the same name, in Uttar Pradesh, India.

Māyāpur—appearance place of Śrī Caitanya Mahāprabhu, in West Bengal, India.

Māyāvāda—misconception that the Supreme Absolute Truth is formless and impersonal or void, and the living entity equal to God.

Māyāvādī—follower of Māyāvāda philosophy.

Mṛdaṅga—two-headed drum used to accompany *saṅkīrtana*.

Nārāyaṇa—Lord Viṣṇu, the Supreme Lord in His majestic four-armed form, who presides over the Vaikuṇṭha planets.

Navadvīpa—(1) present town of Nabadvip; (2) sacred area surrounding and including Māyāpur that was the site of Śrī Caitanya Mahāprabhu's pastimes until His acceptance of *sannyāsa*.

Nṛsiṁhadeva—half-man, half-lion avatar of the Lord.

Paṇḍita—scholar of Sanskrit, Vedic knowledge, and related disciplines.

Prasāda—"mercy"; food or other items spiritualized by first being offered to the Supreme Lord or His topmost devotees.

Prayāga—confluence of the sacred rivers

Gaṅgā, Yamunā, and Sarasvatī, and a major place of pilgrimage.

Prema—transcendental love.

Pūjā—formal worship to a deity with offerings of flowers, food, and so on.

Purī—(1) transcendental abode of Lord Jagannātha in Purī, Orissa; (2) a *sannyāsa* title.

Rādhā, Rādhārāṇī—Lord Kṛṣṇa's most intimate consort, the personification of His internal spiritual potency.

Rāma—an avatar of Viṣṇu.

Ratha-yātrā—annual festival in Purī and other places, in which the deities of Lord Jagannātha, Lord Balarāma, and Subhadrā Devī are drawn in procession on huge decorated canopied chariots.

Sampradāya—sect of spiritual practitioners, maintained by the principle of disciplic succession and distinguished by a unique philosophical position.

Saṅkīrtana—congregational chanting of the Supreme Lord's holy names. *See also* **Hare Kṛṣṇa mahā-mantra; Kīrtana.**

Sannyāsa—celibate renounced life; the state of being a sannyasi.

Śacī(devī), Śacīmātā—mother of Caitanya Mahāprabhu.

Śaṅkarācārya—an avatar of Lord Śiva, who established Māyāvāda in the modern age.

Śiva—exalted demigod in charge of the mode of ignorance and destruction of the material manifestation.

Śukadeva Gosvāmī—great ancient speaker of *Śrīmad-Bhāgavatam.*

Six Gosvāmīs—Rūpa, Sanātana, Raghunātha dāsa, Raghunātha Bhaṭṭa, Gopāla Bhaṭṭa, and Jīva. Contemporary followers of Caitanya Mahāprabhu, all of whom lived in Vṛndāvana, wrote many important books, and became the leaders of the Gauḍīya Vaiṣṇava community after Caitanya Mahāprabhu departed this world.

Śrī, Śrīla, Śrīpāda—honorific titles.

Śrīmad-Bhāgavatam—most important literature of Gauḍīya Vaiṣṇavas, who consider it the topmost *Purāṇa.* It was composed by Śrīla Vyāsadeva to give confidential and definitive understanding of Lord Kṛṣṇa, His devotees, and pure devotional service to Him.

Śrīmatī—feminine form of the honorific address Śrī.

Tulasī—sacred plant dear to Lord Kṛṣṇa and thus worshiped by His devotees.

Vaikuṇṭha—spiritual world.

Vaiṣṇava—devotee of Viṣṇu (Kṛṣṇa).

Varṇāśrama-dharma—Vedic social system of four occupational divisions and four spiritual orders.

Vedānta—(1) conclusion of Vedic knowledge; (2) *Vedānta-sūtra* or the philosophy thereof.

Viṣṇu—Supreme Lord, an expansion of Kṛṣṇa.

Vṛndāvana—(1) topmost transcendental abode of the Supreme Lord Kṛṣṇa; (2) the same abode descended at the site of the present town of Vrindavan, India, situated about ninety miles southeast of Delhi, within which Kṛṣṇa enacted childhood pastimes five thousand years ago.

Yamunā—sacred river that flows from the Himālayas to Prayāga.

Yuga—one of a cycle of four ages that recur throughout the duration of the universe. *See also* **Kali-yuga.**

Sanskrit Pronunciation Guide

Used within this book is a transliteration system widely accepted by scholars to indicate standard pronunciation of Sanskrit.

Long vowels are indicated by a line above the letter representing it.

The short vowel **a** is pronounced like the *u* in *but*, long **ā** as in *far*. Short **i** is pronounced as in *win*, long **ī** as in *pique*; short **u** as in *bull*, long **ū** as in *rule*.

The vowel **ṛ** is pronounced like the *ri* in *rim*; **e** and **ai** as in *they*; **o** and **au** as in *go*.

The *anusvāra* (**ṁ**), a pure nasal sound, is pronounced as in the French word *bon*; the *visarga* (**ḥ**), a strong aspirate, like a final **h** sound. At the end of a couplet **aḥ** is pronounced *aha*, **iḥ** pronounced *ihi*, and so on.

The guttural consonants **k**, **kh**, **g**, **gh**, and **ṅ** are pronounced from the throat in much the same manner as in English—**k** as in *kite*, **kh** as in *pack-horse*, **g** as in *give*, **gh** as in *bighearted*, and **ṅ** as in *sing*.

The palatal consonants **c**, **ch**, **j**, **jh**, and **ñ** are pronounced: **c** as in *chair*, **ch** as in *French* h*orn*, **j** as in *j*o*y*, **jh** as in *bri*dge*h*e*ad*, and **ñ** as in *ca*n*yon*.

The retroflex consonants **ṭ**, **ṭh**, **ḍ**, **ḍh**, and **ṇ** are pronounced with the tip of the tongue turned up and drawn back against the dome of the palate—**ṭ** as in *t*u*b*, **ṭh** as in *righ*t-h*and*, **ḍ** as in *d*e*migod*, **ḍh** as in *gla*d h*eart*, and **ṇ** as in *n*e*em*.

The dental consonants **t**, **th**, **d**, **dh** and **n** are pronounced in the same manner as the celebrals, but with the tip of the tongue against the inside of the upper teeth.

The labial consonants **p**, **ph**, **b**, **bh**, and **m** are pronounced with the lips—**p** as in *p*i*ne*, **ph** as in *u*ph*ill*, **b** as in *b*o*on*, **bh** as in *gra*b h*old*, and **m** as in *m*a*n*.

The semivowels **y**, **r**, **l**, and **v** are pronounced as in *y*e*t*, *r*a*in*, *l*o*ve*, and *v*o*w*, respectively.

The sibilants **s**, **ṣ**, and **ś** are pronounced: **s** as in *s*u*n*; **ṣ** as in *sh*i*ne*, but with the tip of the tongue turned up and drawn back against the dome of the palate; and **ś** as in *sh*i*ne* but the tip of the tongue against the inside of the upper teeth.

About the Author

The author was born in Britain in 1957 and joined ISKCON in London in 1975. Later that year, he was formally accepted as a disciple of His Divine Grace A. C. Bhaktivedanta Swami Prabhupāda, the founder-*ācārya* of ISKCON, and renamed Ilāpati Dāsa.

From 1977 to 1979, Ilāpati Dāsa was based in India, mostly traveling in West Bengal distributing Śrīla Prabhupāda's books. He spent the following ten years helping to pioneer ISKCON preaching in Bangladesh, Malaysia, Myanmar, and Thailand.

In 1989 he was granted the order of *sannyāsa*, receiving the name Bhakti Vikāsa Swami, and again made his base in India. Since then he has preached Kṛṣṇa consciousness throughout the subcontinent, lecturing in English, Hindi, and Bengali. He also spends a few months each year preaching in the West. His television lectures in Hindi have reached millions worldwide.

Bhakti Vikāsa Swami writes extensively on Kṛṣṇa conscious topics. His books have been translated into over twenty languages, with more than one and a half million in print.

Bhakti Vikas Trust

Books by Bhakti Vikāsa Swami

A Beginner's Guide to Kṛṣṇa Consciousness

Read this book and improve your life!
All you need to know to get started in Kṛṣṇa consciousness. Easy-to-understand guidance on daily practices that bring us closer to Kṛṣṇa. Packed with practical information. Suitable both for devotees living in an ashram or at home.

A Message to the Youth of India

Youth of India, Awake!
Your country is destined to lead the world by spiritual strength. Understand the power of your own culture, which is attracting millions from all over the world.
Arise, come forward, be enlightened!

Brahmacarya in Kṛṣṇa Consciousness

A "user's guide" to *brahmacārī* life. The first part consists of elaborate discussions and practical guidance regarding many aspects of *brahmacarya.* The second portion is a compilation of quotations on *brahmacarya* from Śrīla Prabhupāda's books, letters, and recordings.

Rāmāyaṇa

Countless eons ago, when men and animals could converse together and powerful brāhmaṇas would effect miracles, the uncontrollable demon Rāvaṇa was terrorizing the universe. The Rāmāyaṇa records the adventures of Rāma, the Lord of righteousness, as He struggles to overcome the forces of Rāvaṇa. This absorbing narration has delighted and enlightened countless generations in India, and its timeless spiritual insights are compellingly relevant in today's confused world.

My Memories of Śrīla Prabhupāda

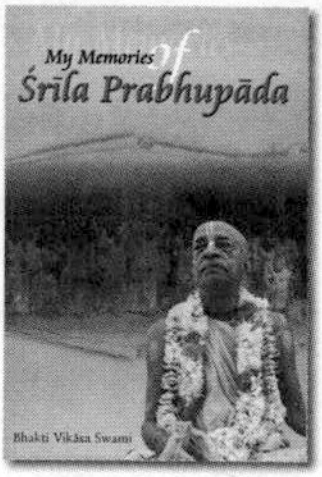

An ISKCON *sannyāsī* recalls his few but precious memories of the most significant personality to have graced the earth in recent times.

Also includes:

- On Serving Śrīla Prabhupāda in Separation
- Vyasa-pūjā Offerings

On Speaking Strongly in Śrīla Prabhupāda's Service

Why followers of Śrīla Prabhupāda should speak strongly, as he did. A comprehensive analysis of how to present Kṛṣṇa consciousness straightforwardly, intelligently, and effectively. Features many anecdotes and more than five hundred powerful quotes.

Mothers and Masters

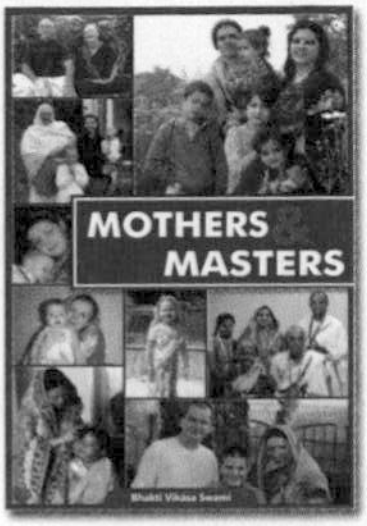

Mothers and Masters presents traditionalist arguments for the direction of the Kṛṣṇa consciousness movement, proposing that we should take up Śrīla Prabhupāda's mandate to establish *varṇāśrama-dharma* rather than capitulate to the norms and ideologies of secular culture.

Śrī Bhaktisiddhānta Vaibhava

Śrīla Bhaktisiddhānta Sarasvatī Ṭhākura altered the course of religious history by reviving and forcefully propagating pure Kṛṣṇa consciousness. His boldness in combating cheating religion earned him the appellation "lion guru"—yet his heart was soft with divine love for Kṛṣṇa.

Śrī Bhaktisiddhānta Vaibhava is presented in three volumes

Glimpses of Traditional Indian Life

Discover the wisdom and devotion at the heart of Indian life. Meet people who were raised in a godly atmosphere and learn how it shaped their character and enriched their life. Explore the adverse effects of India's technological development, the downfall of her hereditary culture, and other causes of India's present degradation.

Jaya Śrīla Prabhupāda!

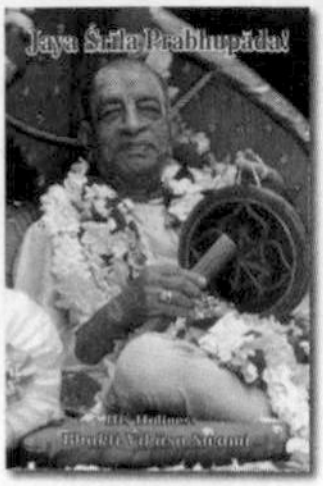

There is no limit to Śrīla Prabhupāda's transcendental attributes, nor do we wish to ever stop describing them. His qualities, combined with his achievements, undoubtedly establish Śrīla Prabhupāda as an extraordinarily great transcendental personality.

On Pilgrimage in Holy India

Travel with an ISKCON *sannyāsī*, including to some of India's less-known but most charming holy places.

Śrī Vaṁśīdāsa Bābājī

Śrīla Vaṁsīdāsa Bābājī was a great Vaiṣṇava who although physically present in this world, had little communication with it. This book introduces us to a personality of such extraordinary, inscrutable character that we simply offer him obeisance and beg for his mercy.

Patropadeśa Vol. 1&2

An anthology of selected correspondence with disciples and other devotees. Packed with realistic advice on how to practice Kṛṣṇa consciousness in a complex world.

Books by Other Authors

Śrī Cāṇakya-nīti (by Patita Pāvana Dāsa)

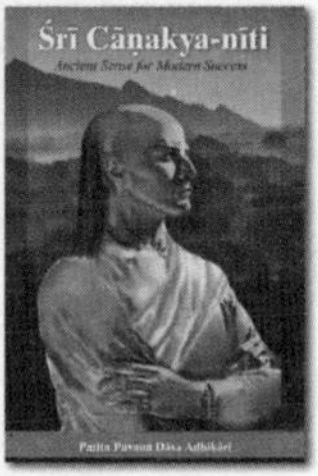

Practically every recorded statement that His Divine Grace Śrīla Prabhupāda ever made about the great Cāṇakya can be found here in this definitive edition. For the modern reader, the wisdom of Cāṇakya is nothing less than the key to a life that is in every way successful, happy and fulfilled.

Rethinking Darwin (by Lalitānātha Dāsa)

In Rethinking Darwin, Danish science writer Leif A. Jensen, in collaboration with leading Intelligent Design proponents such as Dr. Michael Behe, Dr. William Dembski, and Dr. Jonathan Wells, points out flaws in the Darwinian paradigm and examines the case for intelligent design.

Who is Supreme? (by Gokula Candra Dāsa)

Who, if any, among the plethora of gods and goddesses in the 'Hindu pantheon' is supreme? *Who Is Supreme?* tackles this riddle—not with the pablum and word jugglery characteristic of many of today's popular gurus, but with a straightforward and lucid analysis of the seminal sources of Vedic knowledge.

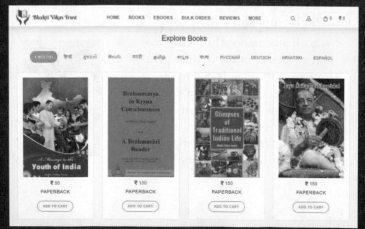

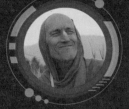

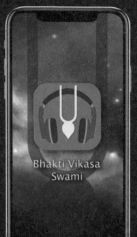